"John has been given battle] against your enemy. This book will show you how to disrupt demonic agendas, prevent an attack before it happens, and recognize the devil's old tricks disguised as new ones. After reading it, you will be equipped with strategies to destroy the various demonic tactics you face daily. This book is a game-changer!"

Sid Roth, host, *Sid Roth's It's Supernatural!*

"In *Destroying Demonic Tactics*, Prophet John Veal offers a profound road map to spiritual victory in an increasingly complex world. From the deep dive into the essence of identity in chapter 1, 'Identity and the Danger of "If Thous,"' to the urgent discussion on the mental health crisis in chapter 2, 'The Current Pandemic: Mental Illness and Emotional Imbalances,' to all of the topics in the chapters beyond, Veal illuminates the spiritual battles we face daily. His insights into the mind's role as a battlefield, the pitfalls of ego and celebrity, and the lurking demon of distraction are both enlightening and timely.

"As we grapple with the pervasive influence of technology, Veal's chapter 'Technology: The Devil Is in the Details' promises to shed light on its spiritual ramifications. The book crescendos with potent strategies such as the power of fasting and prayer, and concludes with a rousing affirmation of the emerging 'Jacob Generation.' This is more than just a book—it's a spiritual arsenal for those determined to overcome. Every chapter stands as a testament to Veal's deep spiritual insight and his unwavering belief in the believer's ultimate triumph. This is an essential read for anyone committed to rising above the challenges and securing his or her spiritual destiny."

Tomi Arayomi, founder, RIG Nation; author, *Eat, Sleep, Prophesy, Repeat*, *The Cosmopolitan Christian*, and *The Occupy Handbook: Your Prophetic Guide for Uprooting Demonic Strongholds and Establishing Atmospheres for God's Glory*

"Spiritual warfare is raging in the earth and will only grow more fierce as we go deeper into the end times. No longer can we get by with a weekend-warrior mentality. We need to stay armored up and ready for battle. John Veal is preparing the Church to destroy demonic tactics that many may not discern. His strategies and solutions for spiritual warfare victory will inspire you to fight and win."

Jennifer LeClaire, founder, Awakening House of Prayer Global Movement; author, *101 Tactics for Spiritual Warfare*

"I admire the ministry of Prophet John Veal. He is a trusted prophetic voice, sent to share divine insight and revelation for such a time as this. I believe this book, *Destroying Demonic Tactics*, will shine light upon darkness and provide clarity by giving you strategies to defeat your enemy. This book exposes demonic lies, traps, and snares, and releases the people of God from demonic strongholds. Prophet John Veal shares personal experiences, as well as the Word of God, to expose demonic tactics. This book is a powerful resource that will equip, train, and activate the people of God. I highly recommend it for your deliverance team, as well as for your personal life."

Ambassador Sophia Ruffin, SophiaRuffin.com

"John Veal's book *Destroying Demonic Tactics* is full of practical wisdom and commonsense, everyday advice that is biblically grounded and actively worked out in his own life, to help you live a victorious Christian life. All believers will have to discover and employ their authority in Christ and the power of the blood of Jesus for themselves in their own unique circumstances, but this book will guide you through the minefield of potential failures so you can step out of whatever difficult circumstances you encounter, with your life and joy intact. Closing our eyes to spiritual warfare won't make it go away just because we don't want to be bothered to deal with our own issues. Read this book and apply its advice to your daily walk, and you will gain great victory over the enemy of your soul."

Joan Hunter, evangelist; TV host, *Miracles Happen!*

"This book is one of the most essential teachings and trainings I have read on spiritual warfare. For too long, believers have been left without strategic training in how to engage in and destroy the works and schemes of Satan and his army of darkness. Once we are saved, we are enrolled in the most powerful army of the universe. John maps out an exceptional teaching in this manuscript, teaching victorious strategies to overcome, prevail, and conquer. Friends, *Destroying Demonic Tactics* is a must-read for every believer. Thank you, John, for this timely and needed message."

Rebecca Greenwood, co-founder, Christian Harvest International, Strategic Prayer Apostolic Network; author, *Authority to Tread, Glory Warfare, Let Our Children Go, Defeating Strongholds of the Mind, Breaking the Bonds of Evil,* and *Discerning the Spirit Realm*

"Once again, Dr. John Veal has delivered a book filled with rich insights about deliverance. In this work, he gives sound biblical advice on engaging and avoiding spiritual damage. Excellent work!"

Ivory Hopkins, "The General of Deliverance," founder and overseer, Pilgrims Ministry of Deliverance

"*Destroying Demonic Tactics* by Prophet John Veal is a must-have for anyone seeking to understand, combat, and overcome the unseen hellish forces that strategically attack the destiny of believers. Veal brilliantly unravels the complexities of spiritual warfare, providing readers with effective strategies to identify and dismantle demonic tactics. This book is not just informative, but is also empowering, equipping readers with the knowledge and tools they need to stand strong in their faith. Whether you're a spiritual leader, a believer in the throes of spiritual warfare, or simply someone seeking a more precise understanding of how to combat the enemy, this book is a game-changer, a loaded weapon in your spiritual arsenal. Don't just read it—study it, apply it, and experience the victory it brings!"

Andrew Towe, lead pastor, Ramp Church, Chattanooga, TN; author, *Breaking the Spirit of Delilah* and *The Triple Threat Anointing*

"My friend Prophet John Veal has written an absolute must-read book for right now. In the current state of the world, we need ministries and books that teach and train us to pray and declare God's written Word and prophetic word. This is the type of book people need to study in small groups. It's rich with insight, Scriptures, and a prophetic flow to help people understand their destiny to a greater degree. Far too many believers have never been taught about warfare and the reality of demonic attacks. This book will help many understand these concepts to a greater degree. I encourage you to read this book, buy a few copies, and sow them into others' lives and futures."

Joe Joe Dawson, Roar Church Texarkana

"The Scriptures make it clear that all believers are in a spiritual battle with the powers of darkness. While the devil is a defeated foe, he continues to wage war against the saints until his final judgment. And while we shouldn't be fearful or overly focused on the demonic, we cannot afford to be ignorant of the enemy's devices.

"In his new book, *Destroying Demonic Tactics*, John Veal equips believers to walk victoriously in spiritual warfare. Using both biblical principles and personal examples, he exposes and disarms the enemy and gives believers the necessary tools to overcome demonic attacks. From the foundation of being grounded in our identity as sons and daughters of God, we can discern and overcome every tactic of the enemy, in Jesus' name."

Jake Kail, apostolic leader, Threshold Church; author, *Setting Captives Free* and *Restoring the Ministry of Jesus*; JakeKail.com

DESTROYING
DEMONIC
TACTICS

DESTROYING DEMONIC TACTICS

8 Supernatural Strategies to Defeat Satan's Newest Schemes

JOHN VEAL

Chosen

a division of Baker Publishing Group
Minneapolis, Minnesota

© 2024 by John S. Veal

Published by Chosen Books
Minneapolis, Minnesota
ChosenBooks.com

Chosen Books is a division of
Baker Publishing Group, Grand Rapids, Michigan

Printed in the United States of America

Library of Congress Cataloging-in-Publication Data
Names: Veal, John, 1966– author.
Title: Destroying demonic tactics : 8 supernatural strategies to defeat Satan's newest schemes / John Veal.
Description: Minneapolis, Minnesota : Chosen Books, a division of Baker Publishing Group, [2024] | Includes bibliographical references.
Identifiers: LCCN 2024010291 | ISBN 9780800772789 (paperback) | ISBN 9780800772871 (casebound) | ISBN 9781493447343 (ebook)
Subjects: LCSH: Devil. | Sin.
Classification: LCC BF1548 .V52 2024 | DDC 235/.47—dc23/eng/20240516
LC record available at https://lccn.loc.gov/2024010291

24   25   26   27   28   29   30   7   6   5   4   3   2   1

First and foremost, I dedicate this and all the books I will ever write to my Lord and Savior, Jesus Christ. It was written to glorify Him.

To my spiritual mother, Ruth Brown: You taught me just about everything that I know about spiritual warfare. You were a demon buster! Rest in heaven.

To my biological mother, Beverly E. Veal: You birthed me into this world, but passed away before your time. Thank you for being the great mother that you were. Rest in heaven.

To my grandfather, S. W. Shockley: You loved me like your son. You were the first to introduce me to the supernatural. I remember all your stories. Rest in heaven.

To everyone who is involved in a spiritual battle right now: I pray that this book gives you answers to your current warfare and provides you with strategies that will put your enemies on the run.

After reading this book and applying the strategies within, I believe you will enter a season where the devil will need deliverance from you!

> Those who see you will gaze at you,
> And consider you, saying:
> "Is this the man who made the earth tremble,
> Who shook kingdoms?"
>
> —Isaiah 14:16

CONTENTS

FOREWORD

The world has been in a volatile state, from conflicts among nations to social and political upheaval, to emotional and psychological challenges plaguing individuals. Anytime we see natural chaos and calamity on an individual or a larger scale, it has a direct connection to what is happening in the spiritual realm. It's clear a spiritual battle is going on for the souls of people. Demonic warfare and agendas are on the rise as the enemy seeks to blind people's eyes to keep them in a state of spiritual slumber and deception. The only tools that we have to combat Satan's diabolical schemes and release the light of God are found in the written Word of God. The Bible is chockful of lessons, stories, and accurate depictions of how to overcome evil and walk in complete freedom. In this book, *Destroying Demonic Tactics*, Prophet John Veal does a masterful job of bringing to light biblical strategies, Spirit-led principles, and effective methods in the Word of God to break you free from the bondage of the enemy.

As an experienced apostolic and prophetic voice, Dr. Veal shows you how to dismantle demonic strongholds that often go undetected in the lives of believers, as well as nonbelievers. Ephesians 6:11 admonishes us, "Put on the whole armor of God, that you may be able to stand against the wiles of the devil." That word *wiles* in the text comes from the Greek word *methodeia*; it's where the English word *method* comes from. It means trickery, cunning arts, deceit, and craft. The devil tries to use these schemes or tactics to interfere with God's will for your life. The enemy's plan is to get you off course and embroiled in bondage so that you cannot fully operate in your God-given purpose and assignment.

Further, the word *wiles* comes from a root word meaning to travel. Wiles target your movement and forward motion. This is because your Christian journey is about changing your direction and path from destruction to freedom. Satan seeks to interrupt your journey and bring you to an altered reality beneath the promise and greatness that God has for you.

Demonic spirits love to fester in secrecy, with their wicked plots shrouded in darkness. Some of the greatest weapons against a believer are hidden assaults and attacks. It's difficult to wage warfare against an unseen opponent. When the enemy remains hidden, he can wreak havoc unnoticed. For this reason, God raises up anointed ministers to expose the darkness, drive out demonic entities, and teach others to stop the enemy's tactics. When the subversive plans of the enemy are exposed, he can no longer operate effectively against you. Light will eradicate the darkness, and you will break forth with the glory of the Lord.

Freedom and deliverance belong to you as a believer in Jesus Christ. They are your spiritual inheritance. God wants you to walk in total freedom from limitations, destructive thought patterns, generational curses, demonic oppression, and anything that could hinder you from fully surrendering to the perfect will and plan of the Father. You can live a victorious and impactful life, despite what the enemy may try to throw your way. Yes, we are in a serious spiritual battle; however, this book will open your eyes to see that you are not fighting *for* victory—you are fighting *from* victory.

As this anointed author expounds on the Word of God in these pages, you will receive divine strategies, insight, practical knowledge, and a course of action that you can apply in your everyday life. You will be challenged to look beyond the surface level and discern what's really at the root of the issues that may be coming up in your soul. You will be inspired to create the right environment for God's prophetic words to come alive in your spirit. And you will be given the strategic weapons to outwit and dismantle demonic spirits that have tried to stand in the way of the new level you are walking into.

As you read this book, don't just view it as an ordinary message. This is a strategic battle plan to help you annihilate demonic systems and ploys that have tried to stop your spiritual and natural progress. Open your heart to receive the instructions of the Lord that exude from these pages. As you apply these principles and methodologies to your everyday life, your world will be revolutionized. You will experience a level of freedom and deliverance that can only come from God.

Joshua Giles, author, *Prophetic Forecast,*
Mantled for Greatness, Prophetic Reset; founder,
Joshua Giles Ministries and Mantle Network

ACKNOWLEDGMENTS

To my wife, Elisa: Thank you for your unwavering support and belief in me from the very beginning. You have held our family together since the Lord called my name. You are the strongest woman I know and a tremendous mother to our three children. I love you now, always, and forever.

To my daughter Jennifer: I believe in the gift the Lord gave you and His calling on your life. When your mother was pregnant with you, during a routine ultrasound, the Lord told me that He was in there with you. He is still with you. I love you.

To my daughter Jessica: You are so much like your mother! With your work ethic and love for others, I know that the Lord will take you far in life. Stay the loving, compassionate, and kind person that you are. Don't let anyone change you. Know your worth! I love you.

To my daughter Jayla: Keep your sense of humor! It's truly a gift from God. When I observe you, I see a lot of myself. Allow the Lord to lead you in all your endeavors. Always be the bright, shining light in the room. You are one of a kind! I love you.

To Brad R. Herman: Thank you for the sound wisdom you have always provided me. You are a true friend who always takes the time to give great advice, answer my questions, and talk about our common interests. I do not take our friendship for granted. I appreciate it and you.

To Jevon Bolden (Embolden Media Group): Thank you so much for all you have done for me as an author. You helped formulate my ideas for this book into a solid book proposal. You have been a blessing to me.

To Lisa Thompson (Write by Lisa): You edited the first book that I ever wrote. Your experience, wisdom, and care have been invaluable. You always take my calls and answer my questions about writing. Thank you so much for your assistance again with this book. I appreciate you!

To Kim Bangs (editorial director of Chosen Books): Thank you for making this book a reality. You made a great first impression on me. I thoroughly enjoyed our initial conversation, and the subsequent ones that followed. I immediately knew that I wanted to be part of the Chosen Books family. You were instrumental in that happening. You are a tremendous blessing to the publishing world, and all are privileged who call you a friend.

To Cheryl Ricker (Dunamis Words): I know the Lord connected us. Thank you for being my literary agent, but you are more than that. You are a friend and sister in Christ. Your support, encouragement, belief, and prayers have been incredible! I'm looking forward to what the Lord has in store for us. I'm glad to be part of the Dunamis family.

To Enduring Faith Christian Center: I am genuinely honored to pastor such a wonderful group of people. Thank you for always supporting every endeavor I've embarked upon. I love you all!

I would like to also thank the following people for their phenomenal support, friendship, and advice: John Eckhardt, Ben Lim, Joshua Giles, Ryan LeStrange, Kelvin Easter, Demontae Edmonds, Rebecca Greenwood, Andrew Towe, Darryl A. Washington, Jennifer LeClaire, Tomi Arayomi, Venner Alston, Sid Roth, Sophia Ruffin, Jake Kail, Joan Hunter, Ivory Hopkins, Joe Joe Dawson, Scott Wallis, Shirley Doss-Williams, Nona McKenzie Parker, Alicia Marie Johnson, and too many others to name here.

INTRODUCTION

New Ages, New Stages

The god of this age has blinded the minds of unbelievers,
so that they cannot see the light of the gospel that displays
the glory of Christ, who is the image of God.

—2 Corinthians 4:4 NIV

Before, during, and after completing my second book, all hell broke loose in our lives! That book, *Supernaturally Delivered: A Practical Guide to Deliverance and Spiritual Warfare*, exposed the various machinations of the demonic realm. Even as I began mulling around the mere idea for the book in my spirit, unusual, otherworldly battles broke out almost immediately. My wife, Elisa, had recently purchased a car. A week or so later, she and a member of our church were driving somewhere, and a hit-and-run driver struck the automobile. Thankfully, they weren't injured, but the car was totaled. Later, we decided to get another car, and seven days after its purchase, the replacement vehicle was also involved in an accident! These collisions were no coincidence, but were part of the enemy's demonic tactics. He wanted to prevent that book from ever seeing the light of day, because the Lord used me to expose the enemy's secrets to the world through it.

The attacks didn't stop with my spouse. The enemy even attacked our children. The worst of his assaults came in early 2019. While vacationing in Florida, I received confirmation that I would be on the popular television show *Sid Roth's It's Supernatural!* to talk about *Supernaturally Delivered*. That same night, Elisa complained of a painful, nagging headache. When we got home to Chicago, she woke me at around 4:00 a.m., saying that the discomfort in her head was so severe that it woke her out of a sound sleep. She asked if we should go to the emergency room. My wife had all the classic symptoms of high blood pressure. I immediately took her pressure—an alarming 200 over 160. This was a stroke-level reading! I rushed her to the emergency room, where she was treated and released.

Historically, Elisa has never had a problem with her blood pressure. It has always stayed in an optimal range without the assistance of medication. I explained to my spouse that I had also faced multiple attacks during this time. Her response? "You're the one writing the book, but we're all paying the price for it." I agreed with her.

The god of this age, Satan, never fights fairly. If he cannot get to you directly, then he may direct his assault toward those closest to you in order to distract you. I don't count it a coincidence that some of my close friends and relatives experienced various hardships during this time.

After all the hell we went through, I told my church and anyone who would listen that I would not write another book on spiritual warfare unless God told me to. His answer is obvious, because you're reading another one right now. I went into this particular endeavor much wiser than before. I now realize that prior to commencing any Kingdom assignment that confronts the demonic realm, like a soldier about to enter the battlefield, we must be prepared for war. Like the coward he is, Satan will attack the most vulnerable persons in your life if he can't get directly to you. As I was writing this, my two oldest daughters were involved in a major car accident that could have easily killed them. Thank God it didn't!

These types of occurrences are commonplace when you have a mindset of bankrupting hell. When Satan attacks like this, people tend to draw back in fear, dropping the mantle or mission God has given them and never picking it up again. This is precisely what Satan wants you to do. He desires to stop your divine purpose because of its potential to disrupt his satanic agenda for God's people. *Don't let him obstruct your mission!* I didn't.

Fasting and prayer are paramount during this process. By doing both, you position yourself to hear God more clearly and build up your spirit. This assists you in knowing what the enemy is planning, having the spiritual fortitude to withstand it, and completing what the devil doesn't want you to finish. Through this book, my intention is to show you time-tested, supernatural strategies to help you defeat the enemy in multiple areas of your life.

The devil has done quite a number on the Church. He has significantly impaired the spiritual vision of both unbelievers and believers. He does this by creating elaborate smoke screens and encouraging division and disobedience, as well as masquerading evil as good. His ultimate plan is to get us to accept a false gospel that is geocentric (earth-centered) instead of theocentric (God-focused or God-centered). He wants to shift our focus from worshiping Jesus Christ to *world worship*. His desire is to convince us to accept a false narrative that exalts social media status over servanthood, a smartphone over a Bible, and a worldly stage over a pulpit. He aims to create such a convincing storyline that it will ultimately spiritually blind us to the privileges, benefits, blessings, and promises that are readily available in the Word of God.

When I read 2 Corinthians 4:4, the verse I quoted at the beginning of this introduction, my focus centered on the word *unbelievers*. This word is not just about people who don't believe in God, but also about actual churchgoers who seemingly cannot discern, accept, and apply divine strategies that could help them overcome the many diabolical trials and tribulations they face daily. Satan frequently blinds unbelievers and creates doubt in believers. He habitually uses seemingly innocuous people, places, and things to infiltrate our homes, churches, and workplaces.

Believer or unbeliever, you don't have to stay blind or doubtful. The Holy Spirit will teach you all you need to know about the promises in the Bible. When storms come, you can stand firm in faith and victory. Loss, betrayal, disappointment, depression, doubt, oppression, and sorrow can cloud our vision of our victories in Christ Jesus. The disciples didn't initially believe that Jesus was the prophesied Messiah. The apostle Thomas would not accept Jesus as the risen Savior until he saw the nail wounds in His hands, put his fingers into them, and placed his hand into the wound in His side (see John 20:25).

Just as Jesus did for His closest friends and followers, God can remove the scales of doubt from our eyes. He will expose the enemy so we won't be deceived. This book will help you see with your spiritual eyes what the *god of this age* doesn't want you to see. It will assist you in pulling back the curtain on satanic counterfeits disguised as godly ventures. Satan has a tendency to infiltrate what can be beneficial resources, such as the internet, media, and social media, in an attempt to undermine the teaching of the Gospel that is currently reaching the entire world.

Through revelation, study, and my own warfare experiences, the Lord has downloaded battle plans and prayers to me that will help you effectively ward off premeditated demonic assaults before they arise. I earnestly want to equip you with tools to defeat an *old devil in a new age, on a new stage.* The enemy of our souls has placed a new spin on his old tricks in both the physical and the spiritual. While his tactics remain relatively the same, the avenues have dramatically changed in our modern era. In 2 Timothy 3:1–5, we learn that,

> In the last days perilous times will come: For men will be lovers of themselves, lovers of money, boasters, proud, blasphemers, disobedient to parents, unthankful, unholy, unloving, unforgiving, slanderers, without self-control, brutal, despisers of good, traitors, headstrong, haughty, lovers of pleasure rather than lovers of God, having a form of godliness but denying its power. And from such people turn away!

Are we not witnessing these very things? As we advance in technology and our access to enlightenment (i.e., the digital era, artificial intelligence or AI, and automation), and as the distance closes in our physical world (which is one impact of the internet and social media), the enemy also advances. While he is not creative enough to come up with anything entirely new, he modifies his weapons to meet every level humanity advances to in each new era. We should not be "ignorant of his devices" (2 Corinthians 2:11). When we are uninformed, we will not discern his devices.

The devil utilizes things that we would not readily think of as demonic tools of destruction. In the chapters ahead, we will address six demonic tactics and weapons at work in new ways in this new era:

1. Identity confusion, the result of believing the enemy's "if thous"
2. Mental illness and emotional imbalance
3. Suicide and death
4. The pride of life and the *spirit of mammon* in the form of ego, celebrity, and the relentless chasing of material wealth
5. Distraction
6. The inappropriate or illicit use of technology

As a believer, you are already a threat to the kingdom of Satan. But you become more of a threat when you grab hold of the authority you've been given by Jesus Christ "over all the power of the enemy" (Luke 10:19). That alone is reason enough to be excited. Do you know when the devil fears you the most? It's not when you get born again. It's when you start to walk in your God-given assignment and authority. Satan will use every ploy possible to dissuade you from reaching it. But through this book, you will be equipped with a custom, supernatural combination of the following eight spiritual weapons to help you destroy the demonic activity of this age at work in your life. These weapons consist of:

1. Cutting soul ties.
2. Avoiding occult activities at all costs, especially those with an upgraded, modern twist.
3. Fasting and prayer.
4. Guarding your mind—taking control of your thought life and gaining the strength to stop entertaining demonic thoughts.
5. Protecting your hearing: What/whom are you listening to?
6. Being careful of your environment: You can't go everywhere, and everything can't share space with you.
7. Cleaning house: Don't allow demons to enter, or especially live in, your home or church.
8. Abiding in Christ: Read the Word and meditate on it, pray without ceasing, pray in the Spirit, worship, and assemble with other believers.

These eight actions, applied correctly against the six demonic tactics I identify in this book, will give you an edge over the enemy and help you realign with God's plan for your life. I love how these supernatural strategies add up to the number 8, which biblically means *a new beginning*. I want this book to provide a new beginning for those who are demonically bound, oppressed, and depressed, so they can be free of the demonic shackles that have held them in bondage for far too long. Through personal stories, biblical illustrations, prophetic revelation, and cultural analysis, in each chapter I will reveal:

- Inside information and insight: how each demonic strategy works in our individual lives, culture, and the Church.
- Your battle plan: how to apply specific Bible-based strategies to dismantle and destroy each demonic act and walk in victory, live out your destiny, and stand for God in the evil day. "Therefore take up the whole armor of God, that you may be able to withstand in the evil day, and having done all, to stand" (Ephesians 6:13).
- Your battle prayer: prophetic deliverance prayers, decrees, and declarations that you need to confess and speak aloud. These will build your faith and affirm your position in God, helping you overcome each of the enemy's tactics.

God has given you an arsenal of weapons that will work against each of the demonic spirits I will expose in this book. To help you employ these weapons, each chapter will end with a special section I have titled "Your Battle Plan," which outlines supernatural strategies for defeating the demonic. Because no spiritual battle plan is complete without prayer, each chapter also ends with a powerful part called "Your Battle Prayer," a set of prayers or pronouncements that will build your faith and secure your victory in Jesus. God has shown me that prayer is one of the most neglected weapons in our spiritual military hardware. We won't neglect it here! We have the power and authority through Jesus Christ to stop Satan's attempts to wreck, disturb, or delay our obligations that were predestined by the Lord. After reading this book and applying the strategies you will find within, I believe you will enter a season where *the devil will need deliverance from you.* Like Jacob in Scripture, you will wrestle, yet you will prevail.

Identity and the Danger of "If Thous"

And when the tempter came to him, he said, If thou be the
Son of God, command that these stones be made bread.

But he answered and said, It is written, Man shall not
live by bread alone, but by every word that proceedeth out
of the mouth of God.

—Matthew 4:3–4 KJV

"I want to see you, Jesus!" I made this statement some time ago,
but I remember that night vividly. I had only been saved for a
few years, yet I possessed a heartfelt yearning to see the King of
kings and Lord of lords while still in the natural realm. While I
was praying in tongues, lying in bed, this thought of seeing Him
overtook my spirit. When I finished my prayer, I made that declaration aloud, full of confidence, childlike faith, and expectation.
In the darkness of my room, a luminous, cloudlike blue mist
unexpectedly began manifesting at the foot of my bed. It abruptly
began to swirl, illuminating various areas of my bedroom while
occupying the space near my window. It methodically whirled

around what seemed like a nucleus directly in the center. Each time the mist completed its circuit, waves of the Holy Spirit hit me like a gentle breeze with a rhythmic cadence. It felt wonderful!

As I gazed at this supernatural manifestation in awe and amazement, a form—a Man's form—started to take shape in the middle, where I perceived the nucleus to be. I was instantly gripped with dread, disbelief, and doubt. I mustered up the strength to speak aloud, "Jesus?" At once, the form began to fade and disappear, but the presence of the Lord that I felt didn't. It stayed for hours afterward. There I was, at the cusp of seemingly getting what I wanted, but I couldn't handle it. *I almost saw Jesus.*

As soon as I expressed uncertainty, skepticism, and apprehension, the image of the Lord left, but His presence remained. After some time, I started to drift off into an unusually serene slumber, but found myself lying very close to a missed opportunity. The next day, I began to doubt my faith, as well as my identity in Him. I considered the Scriptures I'd read about when the angels of the Lord appeared to people. One of the first things they said was "Fear not." Yet I had panicked. I began to doubt that it was actually Jesus Christ in my room. I questioned my worthiness regarding the honor of seeing Him face-to-face before I got to heaven.

To my complete astonishment, however, I recently found out that others—not just me—have seen Jesus in a blue mist. In his book *In His Presence*, Dr. Tommy Combs describes seeing Jesus in a blue mist as a child, while he was in the hospital. He'd been stricken by a deadly disease and was miraculously healed of that infirmity after his visitation by the Son of God. Evangelist Combs speaks of miracles, healings, and the glory of God all happening within a blue mist.

A False Jesus

I've also read stories of people who have asked to see the Lord, and the devil was more than happy to oblige them. Upon their request, he would occasionally appear to them as "Jesus Christ," but later they would discover it was just a demonic materialization. Before my encounter, I heard about a married couple who wanted to see Jesus. They took part in an experiment where they were placed in a room totally absent of light and told that they'd see Jesus. He seemingly appeared to them in multiple sessions, with a woman by His side. He looked like the description of Christ in Scripture, and the woman greatly resembled Mary Magdalene, one of His followers, as she had been depicted in movies and television. This couple had numerous encounters with "Jesus and the woman" over the next couple of weeks. But at times, for a split second, the faces of these so-called heavenly beings would transform into ravening wolves. This terribly disturbed the couple. Obviously, these beings were not the Jesus or Mary Magdalene of the Bible, but imposters whose true identities were revealed over time. The couple hurriedly dropped out of the program when they realized this and never returned.

"Beware of false prophets, who come to you in sheep's clothing, but inwardly they are ravenous wolves" (Matthew 7:15).

Now do you understand my apprehension and uncertainty about my visitation? It is a tactic of the enemy to create and speak through doppelgängers (lookalikes) so that you doubt your identity in God.

Or on recurring occasions, when the Lord gives you an assignment He has specifically mantled you for, the *spirit of doubt* somehow creeps in to discourage you from embarking upon it. This is one of the enemy's specialties, too. He deploys a demon of doubt to prevent you from moving in the direction the Lord has called you, so that you begin to distrust who you are in Christ.

The Demonic Design of "If Thous"

"If thous" are designed by the evil one to get you to doubt your identity in the Lord. When you don't know who you are in Christ, it's virtually impossible to finish what He has called you to start successfully. These "if thou" statements, or in our contemporary language, "if you," basically originate from the kingdom of hell and challenge your heavenly call so that you ultimately forsake God's instructions. It's fundamentally a scheme of the enemy that's usually performed over prolonged periods of a person's isolation.

Let me give you an example. When the Lord first called me to ministry over twenty-two years ago, I was in a very lonely place. I could be in a room full of people and still feel as if I were alone. During these times, Satan attempted to make me doubt the call by filling my mind with "if thous." He would say things like, *If you were truly called by God, then you would never, ever doubt your calling. If you were really a pastor, then you wouldn't be having meetings in your living room. Tell the Lord to give you a building now. It is written . . .*

In the first year of ministry, the enemy spoke to my mind while I was preparing my sermons. He frequently said, *I don't know why you're studying so hard when no one is even going to show up at your church on Sunday.* On many occasions, he was correct. We had church with only the angels as members for quite a while. During this time, Satan used "if thous" to get me to change directions in an effort to convince me to abandon what the Lord had ordained me to do. He did the same with Jesus. Through it all, the Lord physically, mentally, and spiritually defended me.

I almost gave up multiple times because of so many "if thous" throughout the early years of my ministry. What kept me going were the words I continued to receive from the Father instructing me to trust Him during my process, not to quit, and to resist the enemy at all costs. I'm so thankful that I did! Whenever the enemy attempts to make me doubt my identity these days, I reflect upon past victories gained through the Lord.

In this chapter, I will share some lessons I learned in the "wilderness." As I navigated my spiritual wilderness, I had to keep my focus on the Lord. The more I kept my eyes on Him, the more I could discern my identity within Him. Jesus taught us by example how to stand against the enemy's assaults when it comes to our identity. In the wilderness, Satan endeavored to get Jesus to doubt who He was. I want to show you how to recognize the cunning and dangerous design of the enemy's "if thous" and come out of your wilderness with greater power and anointing to live for God. Matthew 4:1–11 (KJV, emphasis added) says,

Then was Jesus led up of the Spirit into the wilderness to be tempted of the devil.

And when he had fasted forty days and forty nights, he was afterward an hungred.

And when the tempter came to him, he said, *If thou* be the Son of God, command that these stones be made bread.

But he answered and said, It is written, Man shall not live by bread alone, but by every word that proceedeth out of the mouth of God.

Then the devil taketh him up into the holy city, and setteth him on a pinnacle of the temple,

And saith unto him, *If thou* be the Son of God, cast thyself down: for it is written, He shall give his angels charge concerning thee: and in their hands they shall bear thee up, lest at any time thou dash thy foot against a stone.

Jesus said unto him, It is written again, Thou shalt not tempt the Lord thy God.

Again, the devil taketh him up into an exceeding high mountain, and sheweth him all the kingdoms of the world, and the glory of them;

And saith unto him, All these things will I give thee, *if thou* wilt fall down and worship me.

Then saith Jesus unto him, Get thee hence, Satan: for it is written, Thou shalt worship the Lord thy God, and him only shalt thou serve.

Then the devil leaveth him, and, behold, angels came and ministered unto him.

This passage appears also in Luke 4:1–13, but for this particular context, I'll stick with Matthew's version. We learn that Jesus was led by the Spirit into the wilderness to fast for forty days and nights and to be tempted by the devil. God instructed Jesus to go there, knowing He would face an extraordinary test.

Notice that Satan appears when he thinks Jesus is at His weakest physically. But despite this, Jesus was spiritually at His strongest. The devil came when Jesus was hungry. He was empty in the flesh, but full in the Spirit. Satan applies the same tactics today. Whenever we appear to be at our weakest, the devil is at his strongest, amping up the warfare against our lives. He primarily does this by offering carnal or worldly possessions that he indirectly or directly proposes. In the Scripture I just quoted, before the devil presents Jesus with anything, he starts off with "if thou." Before making his pitch to get Jesus to bow down and worship him, he tries to create doubt in our Lord. He would win if he could get Jesus to renounce His divinity and identity.

In actuality, the devil doesn't stop with "if thou." He initially says to Jesus, "If thou be the Son of God" (verse 3). We *know* Jesus is God's Son; Satan knows it too. He's trying to appeal to Jesus' humanity, while testing His divinity at the same time. He's trying to plant multiple seeds of doubt in the human or natural side of Christ, knowing that the spiritual or supernatural part is impregnable. Keep in mind that the human side of the Lord was depleted, but the spiritual side was satiated.

The word *be* means "to exist" or "to take place."[1] As Hamlet put it, "To be or not to be, that is the question." One of the synonyms of *be* is *endure*. The enemy sought to get Jesus to doubt His very existence as God's Son, and he came against Jesus' level of endurance—His ability to be who He was and stand in the truth of His identity while in the wilderness. Lucifer tells Jesus repeatedly, "If thou be the Son of God, do this!" "If thou be the Son of God, do that!" He intended to get Jesus to prove who He was, when Jesus didn't have to prove it because He knows who He is called to be. Glory! The lord of the underworld still utilizes this strategy against us in this age. He does this to get you to doubt whatever God has said you are, can do, or will become.

The Word Is Your Weapon!

In Matthew 4:1–11, during the three-part temptation Satan presented, Jesus responded based on the Word of God. When you are tempted by the enemy, the words of the Bible should also be your response. Word knowledge, memorization, and application should be included in your daily spiritual practice as you build your spiritual war chest when it comes to destroying this demonic tactic.

The Lord responded to Satan's "if thou" with "thou shalt," which means "you will." Each of Jesus' "you wills" was undergirded by Scripture. It's worth mentioning that Jesus replied to Satan using Deuteronomy 6:13 and 6:16. Satan quoted Scripture mainly from Deuteronomy 6:16 and Psalm 91:11–12, but added his own words or omitted some of God's words. He has a habit of misquoting biblical verses and twisting their purpose.

When you attack Satan with Scripture, like Jesus, you will win every time. You will overcome the adversity that you may be going through at this very moment. Unfortunately, some preachers have gotten so far away from the Bible these days, which is a huge mistake. A good deal of the messages I've heard sounded more like motivational speeches than Word-based sermons. That's why much of what we hear in some churches or online lacks the Lord's anointing, endorsement, and power. The Bible tells us we can't serve God and mammon, or wealth (see Matthew 6:24). I believe our concentration has shifted as some ministers of the Gospel lead us to seek God's hand over His face, His provision over His presence. My main point is to let you know that the Word of God is your weapon. The enemy cannot stand against it. "For the word of God is living and powerful, and sharper than any two-edged sword, piercing even to the division of soul and spirit, and of joints and marrow, and is a discerner of the thoughts and intents of the heart" (Hebrews 4:12).

"It Is Written"

Satan cannot handle the "it is writtens" that you have available to you when you simply read, hear, memorize, and study the Bible. You must internalize God's Word, allowing it to become an intricate part of your being. Here's how you do this: "You shall meditate in it day and night, that you may observe to do according to all that is written in it. For then you will make your way prosperous, and then you will have good success" (Joshua 1:8).

Yet if there is good success, there has to be bad success. I define bad success as success that Satan makes happen for a person in order to keep him or her in bondage. If Jesus had given in to the temptation and accepted the devil's offer, we would have all been lost.

At times, we can get what we want by exerting our human-made power. The resulting success is usually temporal, not eternal. Just because someone is successful in life doesn't necessarily mean that the Lord has blessed him or her. Because of their prosperity, many people will never turn to the Lord. The enemy's plan is to bless you to keep you.

That's why adversity is good for you. That's why you should praise God for challenging times. Sounds crazy, right? Adversity is meant to strengthen your character, resolve, and identity in God. The Lord wouldn't allow you to go through it if He didn't plan to bring you out of it. Remember, you can't have a testimony without a test. Navigating trouble is likely to produce patience, but only if you allow it to. This happens when you give God the glory throughout your wilderness experience. That's what Jesus did. He glorified God by using His inspired words to combat the enemy. Know that "the testing of your faith produces patience.

But let patience have its perfect work, that you may be perfect and complete, lacking nothing" (James 1:3–4).

In Scripture, Job models a response to adversity that we all should take note of. His wife came to him, saying that he should curse God and die because of all their sufferings and losses. His response? "Job replied, 'You talk like a foolish woman. Should we accept only good things from the hand of God and never anything bad?' So in all this, Job said nothing wrong" (Job 2:10 NLT).

Job and his wife had been through hell. Yet he maintained his integrity and consciously chose to accept both the difficult and the beneficial from the Lord. Please understand that, as in the case of Job, the devil cannot attack you as a believer without the Lord's permission. What you're going through now is on purpose and for a purpose. Keep in mind, God wouldn't have allowed it if He thought you couldn't handle it. You've got this! You must learn the Word of God and apply your life to the Word. You do this by living your Christian life as a reflection of the concepts and precepts within the Holy Bible. In essence, your life should be found within the Word of God. This will help you through your wilderness experience.

The next time Satan comes for you, come for him. Hit him in the eye with the Word! The only way you can do that is if you know the Word. In this new age, it's a sad commentary that some believers have abandoned Scripture, replacing it with theatrics, entertainment, and, as I previously mentioned, purely motivational content. Dr. Charles Stanley, who sadly passed away on April 18, 2023, always emphasized staying in God's Word and never getting too far away from it. He said, and I quote,

I'm going to be meditating upon the Word of God, which means I read it, I ask Him what it means to me, I'm not going to get in a hurry, I'm going to apply it to my life, and ask Him to show me, "What are you saying in this passage?" . . . I'm going to meditate carefully, and I think oftentimes when you do it, privately.[2]

The Wilderness Test

What Dr. Stanley did is precisely what you and I should do. Throughout Scripture, Jesus often meditated or prayed privately. He did this right after being baptized by John the Baptist (see Matthew 3:13–17). He was led by God into the wilderness, a place that provided His private meditation time with the Father, until the enemy rudely interrupted it. At times, Jesus also left the disciples to meditate or pray privately: "And when He had sent the multitudes away, He went up on the mountain by Himself to pray. Now when evening came, He was alone there" (Matthew 14:23).

The Spirit instructed Jesus to go into the wilderness. He was physically alone there, but spiritually God was always with Him. In fact, Jesus was and is one with the Father (see John 10:30). Don't despise times of isolation. This is when the Lord's voice is the loudest. It's also where Satan will try to get you to doubt your identity ("if thous"), especially when no one else is around from whom you can get sound, godly wisdom. The devil likes to talk to you when you're alone with your thoughts. He's a master manipulator. Just as he did with Eve in Genesis 3, he routinely twists God's words and Scripture to establish his lies and make them appear trustworthy. When he tries to use the Word in a distorted form on you, use it correctly on him.

In a place of solitude, you will often gain some of the most significant revelations of your life concerning the plots and plans of the enemy. After your time in the wilderness ends, then rejuvenation comes. So endure the dry, barren places because water (life) will soon arrive. After Jesus was tested in the wilderness, a time of refreshing came right after He passed His spiritual exam. In Matthew 4:11, the devil left in defeat, and the angels ministered to Jesus. Only after overcoming these temptations could our Lord perform miracles.

I sincerely believe the same will happen to you, but you must first pass your individual tests. When you do, the enemy will flee, and you will begin to see more of the miraculous because Satan won't be around to stop it. The Father will dispatch His angels to war on your behalf. After the warfare, they will minister to you.

Doubt Stopped My Gift

When I was in college, a group of Christian friends and I gathered in a dormitory room and began to tarry (which is to abide, or stay in or at a place in prayer). We were tarrying for the Holy Spirit to come into us with the evidence of speaking in unknown tongues. We must have done this for about five or six hours, but it didn't feel that long. All of a sudden, what felt like static energy washed over my body. I felt a sensational surge of power. It was the best feeling I had ever experienced!

This supernatural energy outside myself overwhelmed me. I spoke in a heavenly language for the very first time, but only for a few seconds. Doubt stopped the flow of my gift. This occurred when I questioned how such a remarkable, otherworldly miracle could happen to such an imperfect, relatively new Christian who still battled worldly struggles daily. I cried that night in joy and disappointment. In retrospect, I felt that the Holy Spirit got on me, but not entirely in me.

Let me explain. While the Lord's power, majesty, and presence lingered all night in that dormitory room, the gift ceased. It's similar to what I described to you at the beginning of this chapter, when Jesus started to appear in my room. When the seemingly imminent manifestation of Jesus disappeared due to my doubt, I still felt His intangible presence long after. Likewise, the Comforter, the Holy Spirit, didn't fully manifest Himself in my life until later.

Subsequently, I backslid, falling away from the Lord for about thirteen years. I eventually rededicated myself to God and was filled with the precious Holy Spirit. When I tarried at that later time for the Holy Spirit, I had no doubt that I could receive Him because I honestly loved Jesus and still do, to this very day. I also learned that doubt will truly cause you to go without.

Fractured Identity

First, I want to define the word *identity*. The *Britannica Dictionary* states that is is "someone who is."[3] The word *fracture* means to break. In this season, the enemy's goal is to fracture or rupture who you are. He does this through seemingly never-ending tragedies, trials, and terrors. But the Lord has destined you to triumph over it all. One of the weapons that Satan uses, especially today, is other people. He uses their criticisms, opinions, harsh words, and the like.

This kind of onslaught is especially prominent on social media. I will delve more into technological warfare in chapter 7, but I have seen the victims—and been a victim—of such attacks. At times, these attacks are so vicious that individuals who once followed the Lord start questioning who He is because they don't know who they are in Him. People end up doubting who God is because they see how some who claim to represent Him have viciously attacked others on social media. They think, *If that's God, then I don't know Him. I don't want to know Him!* To protect themselves, they vow to separate from all things associated with Him. In truth, they are deceived by false images the enemy tries to portray through others who are in error. When we don't know the truth, we doubt God and eventually lose sight of who we are in Him.

When you don't know your place in the King (God), you will probably question the Kingdom, creating a distorted focus. Your attention shifts from eternal goals to finite ones. The "Thingdom" (worldly things) becomes more important than the *Kingdom*, causing a pivot in your identity. This shift usually results in a sort of brokenness of the soul. This strategy of the evil one is really to steal your focus off of what your identity in God dictates you should do. Sometimes the best deliverance you can receive is deliverance from people. Don't let anyone or anything break you. You can't afford to question your identity because of someone else's opinion, confirmation, or affirmation, especially during unremarkable seasons of your life. Your resolve must be unflappable, unmovable, and unshakable.

Jesus knew His identity, and so should we. That way, when the enemy tries to get us to doubt it, he can't. Your identity is hidden in the Lord. When you realize that, it cannot be shaken. He gives you this confidence. Who you are in Him needs to be unshakable. You must be so confident in that fact that nothing and nobody can convince you otherwise. Author and former atheist Alicia Britt Chole wrote in her book *Anonymous*, "In each season of hiddenness, our sense of value is disrupted. Stripped of what others affirmed in us. What grows in anonymous seasons? An unshakable identity. . . . Jesus developed an unshakable sense of identity that enabled him to not be manipulated by human affirmation and flattery."[4]

Knowing your identity in God equates to being part of Him because your identity is hidden in Him. When you stand firm on the unshakable fact that you reside on the foundation of faith, you will be strong and perform exploits for the benefit of the Kingdom. Say this aloud: "My identity in God is unshakable." This is your season not only to know the Lord but to do exploits for the Kingdom. "The people who know their God shall be strong, and carry out great exploits" (Daniel 11:32).

Increase Your Ability to Hear God

When it comes to our hearing navigation, it's important that we know how to stop listening to the enemy and start listening to God. The enemy of your soul is a master of disguise regarding his visage and sound. When he speaks to you, it will probably be with a soothing voice, not an evil growl. Satan would rather augment doubt over fear in you, because you can't have one without the other. These two spirits enjoy a symbiotic relationship. Where you find fear, doubt is close by. They work in tandem. Their mission is to keep you at a level so you never rise to become who the Lord called you to be.

In my travels as an itinerant minister, I've seen many people called, but not chosen (see Matthew 22:14). They're not chosen because they doubt the call, so they don't fully walk in or answer it. Lucifer is intelligent enough to know this. This is why knowing the voice of the Lord is so important today. It evicts insecurity from your mind, spirit, and body, and it moves your new tenant in—security. Intimately knowing God's voice breeds confidence because you don't have to wonder who's speaking to you.

In 2021, I created an online class to help people hear the voice of God. It was my first formal teaching on the internet, and the devil fought me like crazy. That's how I knew I was on to something that was of the Father. Whenever the enemy fervently fights what you're doing, it's probably ordained by the Lord. Many who took the course reported hearing the Father much more clearly.[5] Some even reported having angelic encounters.

From time to time in these pages, I may stop and relate to you a word or insight I sense that the Lord is sharing with us about a particular topic. This is hearing the Lord's voice in operation, in case you are unfamiliar with prophetic gifts. It's one way the Holy Spirit guides us into all truth (see John 16:13). Whatever comes forth must always line up with the Word of God, of course. Just now, I heard this in my spirit: *The devil substitutes his sound for God's sound in people's lives to get them to walk down a false path that caters to the flesh instead of the spirit. This is so they will accept a lie over the truth because they think God said it. So many people frivolously operate in gifts, offices, or titles given to them by man, not the Lord, which has caused a form of godliness that denies His true power.*

The devil wants to clog your ears because faith's capacity within you expands when you hear the Word of God consistently. Romans 10:17 says, "So then faith comes by hearing, and hearing by the word of God." And Hebrews 11:6 makes it clear that faith pleases God. Through faith we move Him, know Him, and remove any doubt about who we are in Him. Faith in God and who He has created you to be dramatically annoys and displeases demons. True faith has the power to hinder hellish strategies. It serves as an eviction notice to any doubt that hides within.

Four Prominent Voices in Life

The four prominent voices in your life come from God, Satan, other people, and yourself. These voices vie for your attention daily. To successfully pilot them, you must know the distinct sound of each voice. How do you do this? Simple: You master the art of listening. If you hear anything (i.e., a spirit) or any person long enough, you will be able to differentiate that voice from others. You don't ever have to worry about making any quick judgments about people. Their own words will be their judge, jury, and executioner, at least as it pertains to their presence in your life.

Only a few people truly master the skill of listening, especially to the Lord. God gave you one mouth and two ears, so you should listen twice as much as you speak. James 1:19 addresses this: "So then, my beloved brethren, let every man be swift to hear, slow to speak, slow to wrath."

You will usually find that one of the four key voices—God's voice—will often contradict or directly oppose what your flesh wants to do. The other—Satan's voice—will mostly agree with your flesh. You will have to choose between these two. Our inner voice will echo whichever voice—God's or Satan's—has the most influence over us at the time. A division of voices leads to confusion, and the answer to confusion is clarity. The Lord's voice is clear, strong, and uncluttered, but the devil's voice is filled with clutter (i.e., junk, the cares of this world, negativity, self-exaltation, etc.).

You must be able to align your sound with the Most High. As you do this, you will begin to sound more like Him, averting a potential identity crisis birthed from listening to the wrong source. When you obey the right voice, God's, you will pivot (shift), changing direction, position, or strategy. When you stick with the wrong voice, either your own, other people's, or Satan's, you might follow a path that God didn't choose for you.

Listening to yourself can get you in serious trouble. Ask me how I know! I had to *learn the voice of the Lord* to navigate various adverse situations successfully. I did this—and you can, too—by consistently listening to the Lord during prayer. When you pray, listen more than you speak. You not only will hear God's voice but may be distracted by the enemy's as well. In time, you will be able to differentiate between the two. How do you shift your ears away from the enemy? Identify his voice and stop listening to him. To identify the devil's voice, we have to measure what we are hearing against Scripture. If the words you hear violate the Word of God, what you're hearing is not from the Lord.

A Backward Compliment

From time to time the enemy has spoken to me, and I have yelled, "Shut up, in Jesus' name!" The devil then launched warfare against my entire household in an attempt to immobilize me with fear. He wanted to stop whatever godly undertaking I was pursuing at the time.

When you genuinely know your identity in God, you will start to walk in an unprecedented level of authority when it comes to the demonic realm. The demons will know your name, rank, and serial number in the spirit. The sad part about your new promotion is that these cowardly devils will attack not only you but also those around you. So when you are attempting any type of ministry, or writing a book, or training other people in reference to deliverance or spiritual warfare, you must be prepared for an all-out war against you and your household.

At this very moment, as I am typing these words, the enemy is coming against me. I expected this because it has happened before. It's a backward compliment from the devil. He wouldn't attack if what's being done weren't of God. I needed this sign to let me know that this book will wreak havoc on his kingdom and set many people free, including yourself.

YOUR BATTLE PLAN

Don't hate your wilderness experience! It shapes and makes you who you are in God. You must return to the Creator in prayer and humility to be reminded of your identity. He will reveal this to you as you listen more than speak while you're in the wilderness. Shift your ears away from the enemy and over to God. Learn to listen to God intentionally. In fact, the next time you are in prayer, I want you to listen for His voice most of the time. For example, if you pray for an hour, do nothing but listen for 45 minutes, and only speak for 15 minutes. If you do this faithfully, you will be amazed at how much the Lord will say to you and how familiar His voice will become. When this practice becomes habitual, your ability to identify the voice of an imposter will go to another level.

YOUR BATTLE PRAYER

Father God, in the mighty name of Jesus, I pray that I will be able to identify and understand the many "if thous" operating in my life. Once they are identified, give me the strength, resolve, and courage to serve them an eviction notice, signed by the Holy Spirit, formally kicking out every tenant (spirit) in my house (body) with the last name of "doubt"!

After their expulsion, I decree, in Jesus' name, that I will assuredly know who I am within the Great I Am! I will endeavor to comprehend my identity in you, Lord, through prayer, exhaustive study, and habitually reading your Word. I will be confident of this one fact: If I doubt, I will go without. Therefore, I refuse to doubt anything that you do or speak into my life.

I come against every hex, vex, spell, hoodoo, voodoo, and witchcraft originating from the enemy that tries to keep me from recognizing the Creator's voice. I nullify every outside sound that tries to sway me from the will of the Most High. I declare victory not only in this area but also in every area of my life. I also bind every demon that tries to confuse me about my identity. In divine expectation, I declare right now that I know who I am in Christ, without a shadow of a doubt. I will be more effective as I battle the hordes of hell. The devil will retreat as I hold on to the hand of God as never before. I will decree a new beginning, a new arising, and a new time of dominion in my life!

Father God, I now submit to your will and your way in any and every area of my life that was unsubmitted before. Once I know your will and way, with your help I will never doubt who I'm called to be in you. By your grace and power, Lord, I will dominate my circumstances like never before because I speak your Word over my life daily. Right now, I decree that this is my time to overcome the enemy and have victory in every area of my life. I come against all the demonic tactics of Satan and his minions that have been used against me. I will overcome every obstacle the enemy tries to put in my way. I speak a new day for me into existence, a day in which I will experience the glory of God like never before. Amen!

(Note: Seal this prayer with praise now.)

The Current Pandemic

Mental Illness and Emotional Imbalances

For God has not given us a spirit of fear, but of power and of love and of a sound mind.

—2 Timothy 1:7

In 2020, an insidious disease snuck up on an unsuspecting populace and changed our lives forever. I lost some very good friends and family to this monster that seemed to be birthed from the bowels of hell. It shut down restaurants, movie theaters, and even some churches. During the height of the COVID-19 outbreak, hospitals were overrun with infected individuals, to the point of breaking the capacity of most of them. This was commonplace around the world.

In the aftermath of this pandemic, I had an interesting conversation with my sister, Alicia Johnson, who works in the healthcare field. She began talking about what she witnessed during her daily rounds at the hospital. As time passed, she observed less COVID-related illness and more of a different type of epidemic.

Alicia shared that a great number of people were coming in with the symptoms of a disease that tremendously affected their mind, body, and soul. She said, "John, based on what I've been seeing at my job, the next pandemic that we experience will be mental illness."

Mental Illness Is the Next Pandemic

Alicia's words were prophetic. The mass shootings, suicides, mental breakdowns, and violent actions of so many individuals since then have convinced me of it. Mental illness has plagued the Church and the world for far too long. Sometimes it's mistaken for a demon, especially when deliverance attempts are unsuccessful. Yes, mental illness has a spiritual component, but there is also a natural one. And it's getting worse. Church, let's not ignore it when we see it. Let's get these people the proper help.

My sister's words also hit close to home. Some of my family members dealt with severe bouts of depression during the multiple periods of being sheltered in place in Chicago during the COVID pandemic. One of them, for example, would just sit in her living room in the dark for extended periods of time. All of them showed varied symptoms of depression, but I knew Satan was involved in the equation. This assault appeared to be 50 percent mental and 50 percent spiritual, because a percentage of the depression was supported by medical diagnosis, while the other cause was of unknown origin.

The demon of mental illness can manifest or express itself as severe mood swings, self-harm, suicide, and emotional hurt. This loathsome spirit tends to exacerbate afflictions that occur naturally or genetically. For instance, an individual may be experiencing clinical depression, as diagnosed by a qualified physician. Demons will actually *partner* with the depression that's already there, and the individual's state will worsen. This occurs because disease of itself is demonic in origin.

Further, I believe demons can cause or exacerbate sickness by influencing people's choices through speaking to them (i.e., tempting them to eat unhealthy foods, engage in risky behavior, etc.). Satan is a progenitor of sickness, especially when it's discovered in the mind. If a person hears voices in his or her head, the enemy will increase the frequency, volume, and duration of such events. At one time, a voice might have come primarily from the person's own psychosis, but the voice of Satan is now dominating his or her thoughts. This will continue the more the person allows the enemy to speak to him or her mentally. The enemy does this to alter the person's thought processes in an attempt to get him or her to make terrible, possibly life-altering decisions.

Breaking the Bondage of Depression

Depression increases the longer you allow the devil to speak to your mind. Seriously, the battle is won or lost here. I want to touch on mental warfare for just a minute. I will go into much greater detail on the subject in the next chapter, which is sort of a part two to this one. One of the ways the enemy torments us is by speaking to our minds at the most opportune moments. These well-timed mental assaults are orchestrated to steal your joy, disrupt your peace, and strengthen your depression.

Depression is ongoing sadness that just doesn't go away. It was overwhelmingly prevalent during the height of the COVID outbreak and still lingers to this very day. Demons are involved in augmenting depression symptoms because their endgame is to take your life with your own hands. These spirits repeatedly tell your mind that you're worthless and that life is not worth living. As I mentioned already, whatever you think about the most, you're more likely to do.

Keep in mind, when you are depressed, the voice of the enemy is that much louder. The Mayo Clinic reported,

Depression is a mood disorder that causes a persistent feeling of sadness and loss of interest. Also called major depressive disorder or clinical depression, it affects how you feel, think, and behave and can lead to a variety of emotional and physical problems. You may have trouble doing normal day-to-day activities, and sometimes you may feel as if life isn't worth living.[1]

King David dealt with depression and sadness (see Psalm 6:5–7). Oftentimes, depression increases based on the burdens that you're carrying, and many of them are not your own. In Matthew 11:28, Jesus said, "Come to Me, all you who labor and are heavy laden, and I will give you rest." Allow Jesus to carry all your incumbrances. He is more than able and willing to do it.

The anointing can help break the bondage of depression, especially when demons are involved. The oil, which represents the anointing of the Lord, can remove burdens you are carrying. Check out this verse: "It shall come to pass in that day that his burden will be taken away from your shoulder, and his yoke from your neck, and the yoke [bondage] will be destroyed because of the anointing oil" (Isaiah 10:27).

I can tell if a worship service I've attended, a book I've read, or a person I've listened to is anointed by the burdens that are removed from my life afterward, and by how many yokes (bondages) are destroyed. When dealing with demonic depression, this should also be your litmus test in the spirit. When you're under the unadulterated, untainted oil of the Father, a physical and mental healing manifestation is very likely. It's acquired by partnering with the Holy Spirit and decreeing your freedom in Jesus' name while in these anointed environments. The evil entities that exacerbate mental illness cannot stand against the oil of the Most High. Hallelujah!

Emotional hurt is also a huge struggle for many. At different times in my life, I was so emotionally hurt that I felt as if my heart were literally breaking at that very moment. Have you ever felt like that? For your sake, I hope not. Many people need emotional healing just as much as physical healing—possibly more so. Emotional pain is responsible for numerous people making horrendous, life-changing decisions, including ending their lives. Allow the Lord to heal you emotionally. Don't hold any bitterness or unforgiveness toward anyone.

You will go through a time of inner healing that you'll find in your worship. Worship the Lord your God with all your heart, body, and soul. Praise God in whatever state you find yourself in—happy, sad, etc. The Lord is in a position to mend your brokenness and reshape you. He's willing to turn your mess into His masterpiece.

Don't Die before Your Time!

In chapter 4, I write extensively about spiritual suicide. But before we talk about that, let's first talk about why physical suicide occurs and the principalities behind it. Someone makes the irrevocable decision to commit self-murder for various reasons. Severe depression, intense emotional pain, loneliness, permanent physical injury, devastating loss, terminal illness, and more can bring on thoughts of ending one's life.

Many people have probably entertained thoughts of suicide at some point in their lives. As a teenager, thoughts of self-termination entered my mind on a few occasions. Thankfully, I didn't entertain these thoughts long enough to act on them. As I got older, I realized that most of these thoughts didn't belong to me. The evil one planted such seeds in my head and heinously waited for them to come to fruition. He has likely done the same to you at some point, as he has to countless others, and his attacks start early in people's lives. While the number of youth suicides was rising steadily before COVID-19, they also increased during this time. As of May 22, 2023, suicide was a leading cause of death among young people in the United States.[2]

For years, I subscribed to the school of thought that suicide was an unforgivable sin. But the only unpardonable sin, the only sin you cannot be forgiven of, is blasphemy against the Holy Spirit (see Luke 12:10). If you're wondering if you have blasphemed Him, then it's a strong indicator that you have not. Relax!

Before I continue, here's a disclaimer: What you're about to read is in no way a license to take your own life. As a Christian, your life does not belong to you, because it's hidden in Jesus Christ. You don't have the right, in the eyes of the Lord, to take it.

Today, I feel differently about suicide. Just as people can be sick in their bodies, they can also be sick in their minds. The Lord is loving and kind, and He would take this type of illness into consideration when He renders final judgment. In actuality, the Lord is the very embodiment of love. One prominent aspect of agape (unconditional love) is self-sacrifice. Jesus demonstrated this by going to the cross and dying as an atonement or sacrifice for all our sins. He laid down His life because He loved us so.

Even before going to the cross, Jesus experienced warfare. His flesh fought against His spirit (see Matthew 26:36–46). The cup (the cross) that Jesus had to drink from was very unappealing to Him, of course, but love got Him through. Guess who love is: "And we have known and believed the love that God has for us. God is love, and he who abides in love abides in God, and God in him" (1 John 4:16).

That's right, God is love, and those who make their abode in love live in God, and He in them. In His righteous love, God will save whom He will, and that includes victims of suicide. The devil, who has no love for you at all, is a primary initiator of suicide. He does this by consistently bombarding your mind with thoughts of hopelessness, worthlessness, abandonment, despair, and loneliness. Don't let him! When you maintain a vacancy in your brain, something will move in. Don't let Satan rent a room in your head, because if he does, it will be very challenging to evict him. Guard your thought life. When he assaults you mentally with demonic instructions, cast them down and think as we are instructed to do in Philippians 4:8:

> Finally, brethren, whatever things are true, whatever things are noble, whatever things are just, whatever things are pure, whatever things are lovely, whatever things are of good report, if there is any virtue and if there is anything praiseworthy—meditate on these things.

What the Bible Says about Suicide

You've got a destiny that the Father has given you to fulfill, but the demonic realm doesn't want you to fulfill it. Don't you dare die before finishing what God has called you to do. Suicide should never be an option for a child of God. Yet many of us will contend with it, directly or indirectly, at some point. If that happens to you, come out victorious!

If you have ever experienced suicidal feelings, or if you know someone who committed suicide, you're not alone.[3] In the Bible, we find stories about a number of people who contemplated suicide. We also see accounts of people who actually killed themselves. In addition, we find Scriptures that encourage us not to commit suicide.[4] Let's look at these instances.

People in Scripture who contemplated suicide

- Solomon (see Ecclesiastes 2:17)
- Elijah (see 1 Kings 19:4)
- Jonah (see Jonah 4:8)
- The jailer (see Acts 16:25–31)

None of these men actually committed suicide, even though they considered it. Solomon learned to "fear God and keep his commandments, for this is the duty of all mankind" (Ecclesiastes 12:13 NIV). Elijah was comforted by an angel, allowed to rest, and given a new commission. Jonah received admonition and rebuke from God. The apostle Paul learned that the Lord can enable us to bear all things. He wrote of the trouble he faced, "This happened that we might not rely on ourselves but on God, who raises the dead" (2 Corinthians 1:9 NIV). Paul's encouragement also stopped the jailer from self-harm (see Acts 16:27–28).

People in Scripture who actually committed suicide

- King Saul (see 1 Samuel 31:4)
- King Zimri (see 1 Kings 16:15–20)
- Abimelech (see Judges 9:54)
- Judas Iscariot (see Matthew 27:5)
- Ahithophel (see 2 Samuel 17:23)

Scriptural encouragement against suicide

- Isaiah 41:10 (My paraphrase: Don't be sad! God will strengthen, help, and uphold you.)
- Jeremiah 29:11 (God's thoughts of you will give you hope for years to come!)
- John 10:10 (Jesus comes to give life, and that more abundantly!)
- 1 John 4:4 (The greater One lives inside you!)
- Psalm 55:22 (Cast your cares on Him because He sustains you!)
- Romans 8:38–39 (Nothing can separate you from the love of God!)

If you are dealing with any suicidal thoughts, please dial 988 now. The 988 Suicide & Crisis Lifeline, formerly known as the National Suicide Prevention Lifeline, offers 24/7 call, text, and chat access to trained crisis counselors who can help people experiencing suicidal thoughts, substance use, mental health crises, and any other kind of emotional distress.[5]

Is Deliverance Enough?

Rudy (not his real name) was in church for most of his life. He was an evangelist, heavily devoted to the lost. I met him through a ministry I'd been part of. During one service, the Lord highlighted him as he sat a couple of rows in front of me. God simply said to me, *Watch him.* I did as I was instructed by the Father, not truly knowing why.

On that warm summer night, the gated windows of the building where our church was meeting were open. The pastor preached an engaging sermon, asking his congregants a series of questions such as, "Do you fornicate? Are you participating in sinful behavior? Is anyone here involved in adultery?" Rudy enthusiastically and adamantly answered no to every one of those questions.

Shortly after Rudy had vehemently denied involvement in such ungodly acts, a group of about half a dozen women walked past our open windows, and one, peering in, exclaimed loudly enough for us all to hear, "That's him! That's him!" She pointed directly at Rudy. "He's the one who's been sleeping with my sister, and he's married! See?" She turned to her friends. "This is why I don't go to church anymore!"

The women continued on their journey that evening, and Rudy rose unsteadily from his seat after the service was over. We all went outside with the pastor. Not one word was spoken among us about what had just transpired, but our muted, awkward conversations about various other topics spoke volumes. In my spirit, I felt that the Lord had me watching Rudy that night for a reason. One of the things he had denied was adultery in church, and exposure came immediately afterward. From that night on, he struggled with double-mindedness. Perhaps he had been dealing with it his whole life, but I hadn't noticed. Instability seemed to take over his speech, movements, and mannerisms. He twitched a lot and babbled, and at times acted irrationally. There was a strangeness to him that became more pronounced. These characteristics dominated just about everything he tried to do after that night. His mental state was significantly impacted by his behavior that violated the very tenets of the Word of God.

The word *mind* is associated with the soul in this Scripture: "A two-souled man [double-minded] is unstable in all his ways" (James 1:8 YLT). When your mind is unstable, it's as if you have two souls residing in one body, each with a mind of its own. This creates an imbalance and conflict within people so that they lose their mental acuity and balance in the earthly realm.

After this incident, I didn't see Rudy for years. When I did see him again, he seemed to be dealing with severe mental illness. He often appeared disheveled, disoriented, and off-kilter. It was very disheartening to witness. Sadly, not long after our last encounter, he passed away. Rudy died before his time. A great call on his life mostly went unanswered. The ravages of sin affected his weakened mental state considerably.

I'm of the opinion that the depression, anxiety, and fear that accompanied the pandemic of 2020 played a huge part in Rudy's premature demise as well. Yet what came to my mind was the way his condition was significantly exacerbated that night when his sins were exposed to the entire congregation. With the onset of COVID-19 and its ramifications, Rudy's already disturbed mind lost a great deal of its soundness, tangibly and intangibly, pushing him over an edge he was unable to return from.

Second Timothy 1:7 references soundness: "For God has not given us a spirit of fear, but of power and of love and of a sound mind." Soundness means self-discipline, self-control, and sound judgment, a few of the characteristics found within the fruit of the Spirit (see Galatians 5:22–23). I believe that Rudy passed away due to the evil spirits that entered him through sin and untreated mental illness. Never take a sound mind for granted. It's truly a gift from God. Guard it with your entire being.

Finding the Proper Balance

In cases like Rudy's, we have to find the proper balance between therapy and deliverance ministry. Before Rudy passed away, he was a member of a deliverance church. I'm assuming that he had received and provided tons of ministry aimed at casting out devils. He probably obtained some freedom from those efforts, but it never seemed to last long. I'm sure Rudy needed more than an exorcism or multiple sessions of deliverance.

Let me elaborate. When people are set free from demonic forces, they need follow-up care to address the aftermath of the psychological damage the demons caused. This trauma routinely happens when demons exit a person, but is summarily dismissed in an ever-growing number of churches today. These mentally challenged people can regularly be found in the same deliverance lines every Sunday, yet nothing changes significantly for them.

Persons affected by psychological trauma should see a professional therapist—preferably a Christian one—after being freed from the devil. Therapy for the mind is the treatment of mental conditions by means of verbal communication and interaction. The *Oxford Learner's Dictionaries* define a *therapist* as a person who is trained to treat people who have problems with their mental health by talking with them.[6] Members of my family have seen therapists, and it has, for the most part, been immensely beneficial, especially during the ongoing pandemic.

Today, the rise in demonic oppression and infiltration has led to a subsequent rise in the popularity of deliverance ministry. When it comes to mental health, however, we need a balance between the worldly and the otherworldly in handling these matters.

Both the natural and spiritual realms need to be addressed in order for a person to obtain complete freedom.

As I mentioned earlier, a supernatural prescription to take for your overall health is found in Philippians 4:8. Think upon the things that are godly in nature. Study the Word of God religiously. Read it aloud so the devil can hear it. He hates the Word, and that's a very good thing. One study actually proves that daily Scripture reading at least four times a week can alleviate, to a certain degree, many of the actions that result in depression. It can also improve mental clarity. Look at what consistent Bible reading can do for you, your family, and your church:

Nine Tangible Benefits of Bible Reading

1. Feeling lonely drops 30 percent.
2. Anger issues drop 32 percent.
3. Bitterness in relationships drops 40 percent.
4. Alcoholism drops 57 percent.
5. Sex outside of marriage drops 68 percent.
6. Feeling spiritually stagnant drops 60 percent.
7. Viewing pornography drops 61 percent.
8. Sharing your faith jumps 200 percent.
9. Discipling others jumps 23 percent.[7]

Try reading God's Word consistently and see if you experience these same results. Reading the Scriptures every day can also improve your mental and spiritual mood.

God and Your Mental Health

Does God care about your mental health? Of course He does! Again, 2 Timothy 1:7 says that God gives us a sound mind. But it's the devil's job to give us the opposite. The Lord wants you to be healthy mentally. In 1 Peter 5:7, we are encouraged to give God all our anxieties, concerns, and cares. He will carry those burdens for us.

Philippians 4:6–7 admonishes us to be anxious for nothing. It further states that the peace of God, which surpasses all understanding, will guard our hearts and minds.

In Jesus' words, we are actually called to love God with all our *mind* (see Matthew 22:37). To love Him like this, we must have a healthy brain. One insightful Christian therapist put it this way:

> One of the ways that God shows us that he cares for our mental health is by providing us with the things we need—a great therapist, access to medication, time with Him, a good support system, or all of the above. Loving God with our minds can mean utilizing some of these things he provides.[8]

If you are going through anything at this moment, give it to Jesus. Not just some of it, but all of it. He desires to carry it for you. The Lord wants you to flourish and win the battle with the enemy over your mind. He wants you to prosper even as your soul prospers (see 3 John 1:2). The soul includes the mind (intellect), will, and emotions. God's desire is for your overall well-being. COVID-19 may not be going anywhere anytime soon, but don't allow it to affect your mental state. Give all your mind over to Jesus. (I will address the ongoing battle for your mind more in the next chapter.)

A Word I Just Heard

What follows is something I just heard in my spirit. This may very well be for you from the Lord as you are reading these pages. I sense the Lord saying,

I am now healing you mentally of the emotional pain that you have suffered in the past, and I am pulling you out of it so that

you can function within my will. This torment has displaced you. I am moving you back under the cover of my canopy. Be of good cheer and courage, for I am with you. I've always been with you. My oil is anointing your mind this very instant. Can you feel my presence? I am near you and in you. You are being healed from the inside out. Demons that live in your flesh are being evicted. Habits that you haven't been able to break are breaking now. I desire for you to be healthy in every aspect of your life. That health will permeate your seed, and their seed, and so on down the line. The generational curse of mental instability is forever broken in your life from this day forth!

YOUR BATTLE PLAN

Guard your mind like never before. You can do this by reading your Bible at least four to five days a week, soaking yourself in the Word audibly, surrounding yourself with true believers in the Messiah, getting deliverance, and maintaining your deliverance by seeking out a qualified minister and finding a knowledgeable Christian counselor. Cut off all demonic soul ties (i.e., unhealthy relationships, environments, and situations). Abide in Christ always. Live in the peace of God. When you pray, listen intently to His voice. And lastly, cast your cares upon Him because He cares for you (see once again 1 Peter 5:7).

YOUR BATTLE PRAYER

Father, in the name of your precious and beloved Son, Jesus Christ, I come against the aftereffects of the COVID-19 pandemic that started in 2020. Lord, I come against the demons of depression, oppression, mental illness, fear, and suicide. I come against emotional hurt, demonic chatter, mind control, inappropriate soul ties, and the like. I speak and decree a long, happy life for myself and my family. The enemy will not steal my peace, interrupt my joy, or prematurely shorten my life.

Hebrews 9:27 says, "It is appointed for men to die once, but after this the judgment." My destiny in you is clear, Lord, and I will not perish until it is fulfilled. I refuse to die in my dilemma. My problems will not overwhelm me to the point that I end my own life. You are with me always, to carry my burdens.

Lord, direct me to those ministers and counselors who can and will assist me with any mental issue that I'm facing. I will accomplish that which you have set before me. I will not allow the devil any space in my mind. If he has already taken up lodging there, I am serving him eviction papers today: "Get out! There is no more room at this inn. I am at maximum occupancy because all the available rooms are filled by the Holy Spirit." Hallelujah!

(Note: Seal this prayer with praise now.)

The Battlefield Is Your Mind

You will keep him in perfect peace, whose mind is stayed on You, because he trusts in You.

—Isaiah 26:3

On January 19, 2009, my mother, attorney Beverly E. Veal, and I were having a lively conversation about everything from our church to my children. We spoke on the phone for about an hour. As I prepared to end the call, I suddenly had a strong urge to have her talk to my three daughters. I didn't exactly know why. I just instinctively knew that she had to speak to them that night. She was a bit resistant for some reason at first, but I was insistent. The only one of my daughters who was awake, however, was my oldest, Jennifer. She has the name my mom would have used if she hadn't given birth to two boys. Both of them had a pretty strong bond. Mom and my oldest spoke briefly. Afterward, I told my mother that I loved her. She said the same, and we hung up.

The next day started like any other typical workday. Then I was called into my employer's office within a couple of hours. What had I done? Was I in trouble? No, my boss had just received a call from one of my relatives stating that my mother had been found at her home unconscious, slumped on the floor of the bathroom. I was told that she had suffered an unexpected and devastating brain hemorrhage sometime after we had gotten off the phone.

No! This is not happening! my mind screamed. *She wasn't sick when we spoke! What's really going on?*

Everything about that day was a blur, yet it's etched in stone in the library of my most tragic memories. Dazed and confused, I quickly left my job and drove to the hospital, praying for my mother all the way there. When I arrived, they were just taking her to her room. She was lying on a hospital bed unconscious. Other members of my family also came, but I was the first one to arrive. Shortly afterward, I was allowed to see my mother, who was on life support. With her blondish-brown hair and fair complexion, Mom looked as if she were napping. Those beautiful grayish-blue eyes never opened during my stay that day. Through a torrent of tears, I petitioned the Lord with all that was within me to let her live. I prayed over my mom in unknown tongues so loudly that I'm sure the entire floor heard me, but I didn't care.

Afterward, I was called out of my mother's room for a family meeting with the doctors. They informed us of the massive bleeding in her brain. If she lived, she would be in a perpetual vegetative state. Our loved one would never again be the awesome person we all knew and loved. Beverly had told anyone who would listen that she never wanted to exist in this type of condition. So collectively, we decided to allow them to take her off life support. I'm feeling the tears come as I write this. I returned to her room, still hoping and believing God for a last-minute miracle. I stayed with Mom until she took her last breath and peacefully escaped the confines of her earthly home, to her eternal one.

"I Killed Your Mother!"

With red, irritated, watery eyes, I drove home, thinking what had just happened must have been a nightmare. Sadly, it wasn't.

It was all too real. My wife already knew, but I had to break this devastating news to our children. They were heartbroken.

That night, I couldn't sleep. The devil—yes, the devil—wouldn't let me. He started hollering at my mind, saying things like, *I killed your mother! She's in hell with me!*

He laughed hideously while saying these things, and even more things I cannot mention here. Because of his taunts and devious attacks, I doubted the effectiveness of my previous prayers and decrees.

As a result, for weeks I faced a mental battle I wasn't sure how to win. Satan is such a coward. He will come at our weakest moments and present us with an onslaught of half-truths and straight-out lies to disturb our peace, question our resolve, and diminish our faith. This is one of his tactics. He wants you to embrace a lie instead of standing on the Lord's truth. If you are experiencing this, as I was during that time, you must refuse to believe the devil's falsehoods. His goal is to increase the depths of your despair.

Satan Hates the Truth

The enemy's primary target of attack is your mind. Guess what: He wins that battle if he can take your attention off God and redirect it to what you're presently going through. No matter what, don't let the enemy hinder you with demonic distractions. (We will delve further into this in chapter 6, "The Demon of Distraction.") Stay focused on your Father in heaven, not your current situation. In fact, your current condition is not your conclusion if you keep your mind stayed on Him.

Lucifer despises the truth because it is nonexistent in him. When honesty isn't built into your spiritual DNA, you will lie, even in the house of the Lord. I've witnessed this numerous times in my twenty-two years of pastoral ministry. One of the most challenging places to tell a fib should be the Church. Demons are involved if a person can do it quickly and with little or no remorse. Satan has no problem doing this because he's a liar and the father of lies, as evidenced by this Bible verse: "He was a murderer from the beginning. He has always hated the truth, because there is no truth in him. When he lies, it is consistent with his character; for he is a liar and the father of lies" (John 8:44 NLT).

Lies usually formulate in the mind long before the mouth utters them. As a kid, when I knew I was in trouble with my father for being out past my curfew, I practiced my lie before I got home. Now, don't look at me like that. You're trying to tell me that you never did this? Don't lie! I used my mental processes (practice and repetition) to develop the lie, but the genesis of it came from somewhere in the lower regions of hell.

When someone speaks to you, if you're listening, your mind will mull over what the person just said, correct? It's the same with Satan. He will speak to your mind. If you listen long enough, you will begin to mull over and take stock in his words. Mind you, you may not know that he's the one speaking, because in most cases he will disguise himself as your own thoughts.

One of the first things the devil told me that winter evening in 2009 was that he had killed my mother. Usually, what the enemy says is the opposite of what's actually happening. Remember, this type of warfare starts in your mind. I know I referenced this verse earlier, but it's apropos now: John 10:10 gives us a thief's major assignment in our lives—to kill, steal, and destroy. Satan is a killer by nature. He is a thief by design. He is a perpetual destroyer, at least until Jesus returns. In fact, Jesus came to destroy the works of the enemy (see 1 John 3:8). Hallelujah!

The Dragon's Jargon

As I mentioned in chapter 2, we readily witnessed the devil's attacks during the pandemic of 2020. The dragon will pounce whenever a weakness is displayed, just like a predator leaping on its wounded prey. If you ever suffer loss of any kind, be prepared for the enemy's attack. I wasn't prepared when Mom left us for heaven. I was so engulfed in my grief that initially I struggled with my faith.

Have you ever been there? If I'm being totally transparent, a small part of me was angry with God. I told Him all of the following:

- I'm the repairer of the breach for my family.
- I stand *imperfectly* in the gap for them all.
- I'm the watchman on the wall.
- *Why did you allow this to happen?*

The enemy took that little part that resided primarily in my brain and spread it throughout my entire being. Although those thoughts were fleeting, it was enough for him to torment me with them. It looked as if he were winning the war in my head. For some time, memories of my mother would flood my mind whenever I saw anything that reminded me of her. Has this been your experience after losing someone very close to you? It's tough. This continued for months, and the enemy kept bombarding my thoughts. The dragon's jargon wasn't as frequent as time passed, but it was still present.

Bound by a Spirit of Pornography

Most of the warfare you and I experience is between our two ears. If Satan can get in your mind, your body will soon follow. Regularly thinking about the wrong things can open up portals of access for him. We see with our mind through our eyes. The brain is actually responsible for vision. If someone gets struck on the occipital lobe, the part of the brain that carries most of the visual burden, he or she could go blind. The servants of hades want you to view things with your eyes that are adverse to what is holy, such as pornography. This viewing opens up doors to your mind.

I mention sexually explicit material because people, usually men, typically open this door, whether intentionally or unintentionally. Surprisingly, some women participate in this as well. I'll give you an example. I was at a pastoral ordination service for a friend of mine with three of my colleagues. I was exhausted after ministering earlier that Sunday at my own church. At one point, the newly ordained overseer called my friends and me up to prophesy to the people. We did so, and then took our seats. As I continued watching the service, the Father started speaking to me. He highlighted a woman in the crowd and casually said, *Go minister deliverance to her.*

In my mind, I was saying, *Lord, really? I'm drained.*

He repeated, *Go minister deliverance to her.*

Finally, I obeyed. I made my way over to her and began a conversation. "Can I minister to you?" I asked. She agreed, so I asked her, "What's your name, and do you know anything about casting out demons?"

The woman gave me her name and nodded, and what she said next blew me away: "I struggle with pornography."

In all my years of ministry, I had never heard a female admit that in church. After she said it, I came against the spirits of fantasy, lust, imagination, perversion, pornography, masturbation, etc. Without warning, this woman began to scream loudly, and the next thing I knew, we were rolling around on the floor! I looked around in disbelief, with no one in the ministry coming to my aid, including the new pastor. "Help!" I yelled.

My friends who had accompanied me came over, and we all battled with the demons inside her. Before our battle culminated with the evacuation of those demons, we could see that some of the ministers present were hesitant to take part in the deliverance session, probably due to their inexperience with this particular type of ministry.

We sent the spirits to the pit in Jesus' name. The once-afflicted woman repented of her sins and renounced all associations that had led to the demons gaining access in the first place. This lady, who had looked despondent before, was now radiant. Her face was so clear and peaceful.

By watching pornography, this woman had unknowingly given Satan an opportunity and an entry point. First, he had attacked her mind through her eye gates, urging her to act on what she had been viewing. This may have manifested in a myriad of ways, such as fornication, self-gratification, etc. Her actions had given him access. Once one demon like a *spirit of pornography* gets in, a person's further participation in the sinful act can bring in more. These monsters have a tendency to run in packs. Once evil spirits dominate a person mentally, the body becomes available to them. Give no place to Satan in any area of your life. This is the time to fortify your doors!

Demons Are Squatters

The enemy is always looking for a gate or a door. All he needs is an opportunity, just a crack he can squeeze through. Ephesians 4:27 in the King James Version admonishes us not to "give place" to the devil. By consistently thinking about things that are contrary to the Lord's will, we give the devil place or room. Satan is always searching for a vacancy in our minds. If he finds one, he will take up residency illegally and become a squatter. In the natural, "a squatter is a person who settles in or occupies a piece of property with no legal claim to the property. A squatter lives on a property to which they have no title, right, or lease."[1]

Interestingly, in most states squatters have legal rights after a specific period of time. In Illinois, for example, squatter's rights (or "adverse possession" laws) demand that you live on the property for twenty years before it is legally yours.[2] But in many states—including the supernatural state—it doesn't take nearly that long before a squatter can take possession. Demons are squatters. If they occupy space in your head for an extended time, they can establish legal rights to you that can only be nullified through the blood of Jesus. This nullification can be done through biblical deliverance. In deliverance meetings, I've heard demons actually cry out through an individual "I have a legal right to be here!" and refuse to leave. They are claiming this right based on years of unauthorized or unnoticed occupancy.

For this reason, we must routinely inspect and cleanse our minds. We can do this by maintaining the mind of Christ, as Philippians 2:5 instructs us: "Let this mind be in you which was also in Christ Jesus." When you have Christ's consciousness, Satan cannot penetrate it. When he tries, he will encounter a sign in the spirit that reads *No Vacancies!*

When in the flesh, Jesus' mind was saturated with humility. It was just the opposite of the devil's, which was infested with pride. Philippians 2:8 says that while in the flesh, the Lord "humbled Himself and became obedient to the point of death, even the death of the cross." His whole life was illustrated by this quality of humility, along with gentleness and self-sacrifice, traits that are foreign to Lucifer. Humility begins in and is cultivated within the mind. You can't have an arrogant mind and a humble body, because the body is an instrument of the brain. It carries out the mind's will. So when vain, evil, or useless thoughts enter your mind, cast them down. Immediately begin "casting down arguments and every high thing that exalts itself against the knowledge of God, bringing every thought into captivity to the obedience of Christ" (2 Corinthians 10:5).

Anything that conflicts with what the Lord has already informed you of must be cast down. You must train your mind to think like Jesus. This process might take quite a bit of time, but it can be done according to the Scriptures. Of course, crazy thoughts will visit your mind, but don't let them stay. As soon as you identify one, cast it out. That's what I do, and I get such thoughts daily.

Remember, the enemy wars against your mind because if he wins, he gets your body. If he controls your body, he can influence your eternal destiny in the worst way. Don't let him win. He succeeds by getting you to accept a false narrative, by inserting his disinformation in place of the truth. It's among his most effective battle plans.

Like me, have you ever had an absolutely absurd thought? Did you ever have a nightmare that was so repulsive that you began to question your salvation? In many of these instances, it wasn't your own thoughts or your dreams; these thoughts and dreams were demonically deployed. They were planted in your mind by the residents of hell. Demons are assigned to your life to do these specific things because Satan realizes how important it is for him to win the battle for your mind.

Cast Fear Out of Your Mind

If devils can enter people, places, and animals (like the pigs in Matthew 8:28–34), it's not a significant stretch for them to pierce our dreams. Dreams form in the mind, but occasionally, their source can be demonic. Recently, I had a dream in which a demon jumped on me. Incredibly enough, I had no fear at all. I just rebuked it in Jesus' name, and it left immediately. In the past when this kind of thing happened, I had to tell the demon to go about three times before it left. The problem then was that fear was attached to my declaration. The more you fear the devil, the longer he will stick around.

In chapter 2 we touched on 2 Timothy 1:7 and learned that fear is a spirit. If it's a spirit, it can be cast out. You must do this before engaging in mental warfare with the enemy. Get rid of the fear. Romans 8:31 says, "If God is for us, who can be against us?" If God be for you, He is stronger than anything in the world that is against you, including devils. Daniel 11:32 confidently reads, "But the people who know their God shall be strong, and carry out great exploits." This is something to get excited about!

You're more than a conqueror through Christ (see Romans 8:37). Don't allow any no-good devil to win the battle for your mind. *The way to keep the devil off your mind is to keep God on it.*

> Don't copy the behavior and customs of this world, but let God transform you into a new person by changing the way you think. Then you will learn to know God's will for you, which is good and pleasing and perfect.
>
> Romans 12:2 NLT

Worry starts in the mind. So don't worry when the enemy comes to unsettle your thinking by purposely antagonizing you. He usually does this through adverse situations and people. Refuse to let yourself be annoyed by external issues that are augmented by demonic conversations. The kingdom of hell wants you to worry about incidents that will probably never happen.

Don't be affected by all that's transpiring around you at the moment. It will end. It's your time not to let either demons or individuals make you lose focus on what the Lord has called you to do. Make a concerted effort to maintain your mental focus as you progress into "the next and the new" that the Lord has prepared for you. Don't let negativity occupy space in your mind. Make sure that there are no openings in your head. Be encouraged!

You're on God's Mind

The Lord is thinking about all you're going through today and this year. Rest assured, you are currently on His mind. He is working out your dilemmas and answering your inquiries.

In fact, God is repositioning you out of your story and into His glory. In your new position, *favor* has become your new neighbor, *increase* has moved onto your block, and *healing* has relocated to your upstairs bedroom.

As you remove the demonic clutter from your mind, get ready for manifested miracles. The Lord will send them your way soon. Don't let yourself be discouraged by the picture the enemy has painted regarding what's to come. Stay encouraged! The Lord has already worked it all out in His mind. Now it's time to wait for the manifestation.

As you wait, decree what you expect to see. It's your time. It's your season. God has been on your mind lately. You've been on His mind as well. Prepare for the manifold blessings that are currently headed your way.

YOUR BATTLE PLAN

You must consult God before, during, and after any battle. Keep the Lord on your mind because that will keep Satan out. Consistently cover your mind with the blood of Jesus. Read and study the Scriptures three times a day: morning, afternoon, and evening. Limit your interaction with negative worldly influences like inappropriate movies or unsaved friends (unless you're leading those people to the Lord). If you're able to, fast from all secular music for twenty-one days. It takes about three weeks of consistency to make lasting changes in your life. Allow yourself to be saturated with anointed Christian music during this time. Couple this with the Scripture readings. This will help renew, replenish, and reset your mind.

YOUR BATTLE PRAYER

Father, in the matchless and mighty name of Jesus, I decree that I will win the battle for my mind. Thank you for providing all the supernatural weaponry needed to send demons running out of my thoughts in terror. James 4:7 says that if I submit myself to you and resist the devil, he will flee from me. Lord, I oppose him in my mind. I disavow demonic conversations that I have entertained mentally. I cast them all down. As Philippians 4:8 instructs, I will think about things that are true, honest, just, pure, lovely, of good report, virtuous, and praiseworthy. I will make a covenant with my mind and my eyes to avoid viewing or thinking upon things that will only bring about an evil report.

Father, refresh, reset, and restructure my mind so that my cognitive function operates like your precious Son, Jesus. Forgive me for whenever I have dishonored you in my past thought life. I repent! Help me push out any evil entries. Dad, dominate my mind, and replenish and renew it.

I also break every generational curse that currently exists in my bloodline and affects my mental state. I am a bloodline breaker! Such curses will not affect my children, my children's children, or any generation to come. My mind is covered with the precious blood of Jesus. No demon can infiltrate it. Lord, I thank you that my mind is sound, according to 2 Timothy 1:7. I am winning the battle for the control of my thought life through you. Thank you, Jesus! Amen.

(Note: Seal this prayer with praise now.)

Spiritual Suicide

With their flocks and herds they shall go to seek the LORD,
but they will not find Him; He has withdrawn Himself
from them.

—Hosea 5:6

At nineteen, I accepted Jesus Christ as my Lord and Savior at
North Carolina Central University in Durham, North Carolina.
It was the best decision I had ever made. Not long after, how-
ever, I spiraled into a backslidden state for almost thirteen years.
During this time of disobedience, I was committing spiritual
suicide and didn't even know it. We will get to that in a minute.
Thankfully, at the age of thirty-two, I had an encounter with the
Lord that changed the course of my life. The words He spoke to
me that night changed how I view the ways we can kill ourselves
spiritually.

It was 1998, and I was reading a book called *A Divine Revelation of Hell* by my friend Mary K. Baxter. Sadly, Mary moved
into her heavenly abode on September 13, 2021, at the ripe old
age of eighty-one. In her bestselling literary endeavor, Mary describes her supernatural tour of hell in great detail. Accompanied

by Jesus, Mary was taken there in the spirit and endured a terrifying forty consecutive nights in the belly of the beast. I was so engrossed in her horrifying excursion through the kingdom of Satan that I couldn't put it down. The more I read, the more convicted I became. I softly cried throughout. I highly recommend getting this book and reading it once a year. You most assuredly will reevaluate your salvation, ministry, and calling. (As a side note, I met Mrs. Baxter about five years after I read the book, and she looked me in the eye with the utmost sincerity and said in reference to her divine revelation of hell testimonies, "It's all true.")

With only two pages to go in Mary's page-turner that evening, a tremendous urgency to rededicate myself to the Lord overwhelmed me. The first thing that I remember doing was speaking aloud the following verse as best I could. Trust me when I tell you that my knowledge of the Bible was rudimentary at best back then. I butchered this verse, but mercifully, the Lord honored my effort: "Behold, I stand at the door and knock. If anyone hears My voice and opens the door, I will come in to him and dine with him, and he with Me" (Revelation 3:20).

As soon as I articulated this verse, the Father began to speak to my spirit. He said, somewhat sternly (at least from what I interpreted through my spirit), *It's time to follow me fully. I've allowed you to do what you've wanted, but now you have to make a choice: choose me or choose the world. If you make the wrong decision, the protective hedge [barrier, wall] that has been around you your whole life will be taken away.*

Without conscious thought, I somehow knew He meant that I would be left to my own devices. I could do what I wanted to do, but the hedge of protection that He provided would no longer be available. Please understand that the Lord did not say He would leave me; only that He would no longer protect me. In the spirit, I felt as if His hand would no longer shield me from the attack of the evil one.

God's Hand and Hedge

God's hedge of protection and hand of protection are interchangeable; both are symbolic of provision and protection in the Bible. Spiritually, His hand is our hedge. Let's look more closely at His hand of provision, hand of protection, and hedge of protection. Here are some Scriptures that cover these biblical principles:

Hand of Provision

So I decided there is nothing better than to enjoy food and drink and to find satisfaction in work. Then I realized that these pleasures are from the hand of God. For who can eat or enjoy anything apart from him?

Ecclesiastes 2:24–25 NLT

You open your hand and satisfy the desires of every living thing.

Psalm 145:16 NIV

Hand of Protection

Though I walk in the midst of trouble, you preserve my life. You stretch out your hand against the anger of my foes; with your right hand you save me.

Psalm 138:7 NIV

For the life of every living thing is in his hand, and the breath of every human being.

Job 12:10 NLT

Hedge of Protection

You have always put a wall of protection around him [Job] and his home and his property. You have made him prosper in everything he does. Look how rich he is!

Job 1:10 NLT

Now let me tell you what I will do to my vineyard: I will tear down its hedges and let it be destroyed. I will break down its walls and let the animals trample it.

Isaiah 5:5 NLT

Note that in Job 1:10, Satan is speaking about Job. In the King James Version of this verse, the word used for "wall of protection" is *hedge*. (I will expound more on the Lord's hedge of protection in chapter 7.)

In one online article, author and teacher Jeremy Meyers states, "Frequently, due to sin, rebellion, and the other factors, God simply withdraws His protective hand and allows sin, Satan, and chaos to have their way."[1] At times, the Lord will remove His hand or hedge or protection after giving a person multiple chances to do His will. God will also withdraw Himself (His Spirit) when He has an assignment for us and we continue to run from it (see Hosea 5:6).

God warned me that He would step back if I kept refusing to do things the way He wanted me to. I had chosen to live under a form of godliness that denied His power (see 2 Timothy 3:5), and He was growing weary of me. He essentially told me that it was now or never. If I wasn't going to be about my Father's business, then the Father would have nothing to do with my business. Sounds harsh, huh? That's the way our heavenly Daddy talks to His hardheaded children, and I am one of them!

In Genesis 6:3, the Lord said, "My Spirit shall not strive with man forever, for he is indeed flesh; yet his days shall be one hundred and twenty years." There are various schools of thought on the subject of this verse. It could mean exactly what it says. It could imply that the Lord would eventually wipe out His creation in the Flood 120 years after He made this statement. It could signify that the Father will not always protect us from calamity. Perhaps it's referring to a man's (or woman's) eventual death. Let's go with the thought that this verse is talking about God, who is

Spirit, not always laboring with flesh (humankind). At that time, the Lord was dealing with a large segment of seditious and stubborn people who refused to believe the warning He gave to Noah concerning the impending destruction of the world by water, or the instructions He gave him to build the Ark.

The more rebellious we are, the further our flesh or carnal nature gets away from the protection of God's hand or His hedge. The more we move out from under the Lord's covering, the less His hand or hedge will shield us. In Psalm 91:1, as His children we are encouraged to dwell in His secret place and stay under "the shadow of the Almighty." The shadow represents His presence, peace, power, and protection. In the natural, when light is present a shadow is cast, and you can move out from under the shade's protection. In the same way, it's possible in the spiritual to move out from under the shade—the shadow or canopy of God's presence. To stay protected, we must endeavor to remain in the supernatural shade cast by the light of His presence.

Continuous disobedience to God slowly kills our spirit (life). When God told me to choose, the wrong decision could have meant my spiritual death, which was what the enemy desired. I could probably have lived a long life physically, but I wouldn't be living in God's shade (protected by Him) if I refused to accept His second chance—a chance I honestly didn't deserve. He gave me a choice—live for Him or live for myself.

I replied, "I choose you!"

It was the only response that made sense to me. I said it aloud, with tears rolling down my face. Suddenly, I was refilled. It felt as if I were a half-full glass of water instantly filled to the brim. I found out later that the Holy Spirit had fully moved into my body. John 14:17 let me know that the Holy Spirit had been with me up to that point—but afterward, the Holy Spirit was *in* me (and still is). I will never forget that day. I became more alive from that day forward. Death no longer had any power over me. In fact, that day *death died* and I began to truly live. Hallelujah!

Obedience Is God's Love Language

If I had chosen poorly at that defining moment in my life, I probably would be physically or spiritually dead, or both. I was *killing myself* spiritually by disobeying God. When we are disobedient to the Lord, it can bring demonic torment into our lives.

Obedience is God's love language. When we love the Lord, we will obey Him and keep His statutes. In John 14:15, Jesus said, "If you love Me, keep My commandments." The Lord has established His laws for our own good. When we go outside them, catastrophe awaits.

Obedience is better than sacrifice. The Lord is more concerned about your obedience than He is about what you give Him, whether it be your time, talent, or treasure. When the Father threatened to take His hedge of protection from me, I had lived in disobedience for thirteen years. The further I got away from Him, the less I prayed. The less I read His Word, the more my spirit or will to serve the Lord died. I was turning into a dead man walking.

The prophet Samuel alludes to obeying the Lord and listening to His voice, two things that are crucial regarding serving Him: "Has the LORD as great delight in burnt offerings and sacrifices, as in obeying the voice of the LORD? Behold, *to obey is better than sacrifice*, and to heed than the fat of rams" (1 Samuel 15:22, emphasis added).

The High Cost of Habitual Noncompliance

At this point, I want to focus on spiritual suicide—what it means, how you can avoid it, and how it can still affect us today. We will also explore the relationship between disobedience and demonic torment. Further, we will discover how obedience is a spiritual warfare and deliverance strategy that can bring blessings, peace, and elysian (divine) protection into our lives.

The greater the level of people's disobedience to the Lord, the more access Satan has to them. Habitual noncompliance to God's commands opens portals of demonic penetration. Unfortunately, some living people have become members of the legion of the walking dead—zombies with no spirit, if you will. Perhaps they were given the same choice that I was. Maybe they just continued to reject the Lord's calling, conditioning, and commissioning. Let's delve into this a bit more and look at what it means when someone experiences spiritual demise.

In the 1990s, I was living in a long-term state of rebellion against God. "Rebellion is as the sin of witchcraft" (1 Samuel 15:23). In the Old Testament, the Israelites were told, "Thou shalt not suffer a witch to live" (Exodus 22:18 KJV). If someone continues to rebel against the Lord, that person may be risking his or her life. Now, I was never a warlock (a male witch), but I was definitely defiant. This characteristic could have cost me my life.

In actuality, as you just read, I almost lost the Lord's divine providence because I refused to submit to His total will for my life. If I had not acquiesced, I ultimately would have reworked the trajectory of my life—and not for the better. In the Old Testament, Jerusalem murdered and stoned God's prophets. The Lord's heart was to protect His people as a nation, but He couldn't do it because they wouldn't let Him. As Jesus cried out when He came, "O Jerusalem, Jerusalem, the city that kills the prophets and stones God's messengers! How often I have wanted to gather your children together as a hen protects her chicks beneath her wings, but you wouldn't let me" (Matthew 23:37 NLT).

God wants to protect His children. Disappointingly, many today have moved out from under the hand or hedge of the Lord in pursuit of earthly pleasures that are mostly short-lived. In their rush, they knowingly or unknowingly abandon their covering. Whenever we do this, we are *executing* our own spirits. It has been reported that for each cigarette you smoke, you take a minute off your life. In my humble opinion, habitual sin does the same thing to a believer (see Romans 6:23). Noncompliance with God's will and ways has an extremely high cost.

What Is Spiritual Death?

Before we proceed, I want to make sure that you know how I'm using the term *spirit* here. In this chapter, I'm using *spirit* in reference to a person's will—something that can be activated or stirred up, a person's breath or personality. Let's look at some definitions of the word *spirit*, with scriptural backup for each one.[2] In the Old Testament, the Hebrew word for "spirit" is *ruah*. Basically, it means wind (see Isaiah 7:2; Genesis 1:2; 3:8; Exodus 10:13; 14:21), but it also often means breath (see Isaiah 42:5; Ezekiel 37:9–10; Job 19:17). It can likewise refer to the will. In Ezra 1:5, those whose spirits God had stirred up had the will to rebuild the temple. In Numbers 14:24, Caleb had a different spirit from the rest of the spies and therefore assessed differently the possibility of conquering the land. *Pneuma* (*pneu'ma*) is the New Testament counterpart to *ruah*. Here, too, it can occasionally mean wind or breath (see John 3:8; Matthew 27:50; 2 Thessalonians 2:8). But it is generally translated "spirit," or that dimension of our human personality wherein we can have a relationship with God (see Mark 2:8; Acts 7:59; Romans 1:9; 8:16; 1 Corinthians 5:3–5).

As we will see, you can experience a spiritual death while yet in the land of the living. I almost did. A person who is spiritually dead has no life by which he or she can respond to spiritual things, much less live a spiritual life. No amount of God's love, care, and words of affection will draw a response. A spiritually dead person is alienated from God, and therefore alienated from living a spiritual life. He or she has no capacity to respond. As the great Scottish commentator John Eadie said, "It is a case of death walking."[3] Men apart from God are spiritual zombies, the walking dead who don't know they are dead. They go through life's motions, but do not possess life. According to John MacArthur in his commentary on Ephesians 2,

> In the state of spiritual death, the only walking or living a person can do is **according to the course of this world, according to the prince of the power of the air, of the spirit that is now working in the sons of disobedience.** *Kosmos* (**world**) does not here represent simply the physical creation but the world order, the world's system of values and way of doing things—the world's **course.** And as Paul makes clear, the **course of this world** follows the leadership and design of Satan, **the prince of the power of the air.**[4]

When you're spiritually dead, you're not moved by activities within the spirit realm. As I mentioned, people apart from God are spiritual zombies, or the walking dead. They are bound by the course of this world, not by His Spirit. They end up "tithing their resources to the devil" because he, by default, becomes their prince (see Ephesians 2:2). Not only that, but they've given Satan a place or an opening into their lives for so long that he has become rooted or grounded in them. Ephesians 4:26–27 warns us not to give him an opportunity to get a bridgehead or a toehold so he can induce us to sin.

Remember, sin ushers in death, but the death may take place spiritually before it happens physically. The Lord gave us all a free will. We can choose to follow Him, or choose the world (*kosmos*) and all its values, morals, and systems.[5] At present, the devil runs the world (see John 12:31). We see evidence of this anytime we watch the nightly news. He is the god of this world (age), according to 2 Corinthians 4:4. To guard against his temporary rule, we must always be sensitive to the spiritual aspects of our Lord and ourselves.

Disobedience Allowed Demons to Enter

Years ago, when I was bound by sin, my response to spiritual things was at an all-time low. Have you ever been there? I didn't want to go to church. I had a very shallow prayer life. In my eyes, just about every preacher I knew was a con man. I had a love-hate relationship with Christianity; a significant part of me loved it, but the demons inside me detested it.

My brother Jeff made Jesus his Lord right before my rededication and presented the Gospel to Elisa and me every chance he got. You know what I'm talking about, right? He was really getting on our nerves!

One night, Jeff was ministering to us, and something deep within me hated him for it. It shocked me because I love my little brother. After he left, I felt terrible. Later, I realized that I had gotten so far away from my relationship with the King that I had allowed demonic spirits to take up residency in me. It wasn't me who despised Jeff that evening; it was Satan. Fortunately, subsequent deliverance sessions and true salvation freed me of the devil's grip on my soul.

Honestly, has this ever happened to you? Did you ever feel something that was so foreign to you that you knew it came from the pits of hell? I have felt that more than once. This is one of the reasons deliverance must be maintained in order for it to be retained. Satan was trying to get me to die spiritually to God. The manner of my death would have been spiritual suicide.

My case was very similar to King Saul's when he made the ill-fated decision to disobey the word of the Lord that the prophet Samuel gave him. Saul's decision cost him the kingdom and the Spirit of the Most High (see 1 Samuel 15).

Saul was spiritually dead to the Lord. As a result, God tore the kingdom of Israel from him and never spoke to him again while he was alive. The Lord's words are life and spirit (see John 6:63). Whenever Saul inquired of the Lord directly through the prophets, He would not answer him by dreams or any other way. Because of the absence of God's voice, Saul consulted a witch (see 1 Samuel 28).

Another result of King Saul's disobedience was that he no longer enjoyed the Lord's protection. The Philistines killed his sons (Jonathan, Abinadab, and Malchishua) in battle, and before these enemies could get to Saul, he killed himself by falling on his own sword (see 1 Samuel 31).

Yet Saul had died spiritually years before he died naturally. Unfortunately, we can experience this type of death when we continue to live outside the will of God. If Saul had done what the Lord had asked him to do in the first place, perhaps he could have avoided his fate. Obedience is key to avoiding spiritual death.

What Is Spiritual Suicide?

Spiritual suicide is the killing of the part of yourself that serves God. You do this when you repeatedly abandon the missions, mandates, and ministry the Lord has given you to do while on earth. Tragically, this is the reason so many people die before their time. As I alluded to earlier, the Father gives them chance after chance after chance to serve Him, but each time, they refuse. Romans 8:9 reminds us that "if anyone does not have the Spirit of Christ, they do not belong to Christ" (NIV). These people slowly commit suicide spiritually before actually passing in the flesh.

Take into account that the only reason you're alive and reading this is because God has a purpose for your life. When people commit spiritual suicide, they have no interest in things of the Spirit, including what the Lord has commanded them to do. The material world and all it offers dominate their lives. They don't have the urge to go to church, pray to the Lord, or worship Him. Such people spend their whole lives mainly conscious of their bodies. Their core concerns are themselves and whatever affects them, negatively or positively. Like Satan, self-centeredness is their portion.

Spiritual suicide occurs when we prioritize our will over God's will, combined with consistently rebelling against what He wants us to do with the life He gave us. Like someone who has a reprobate mind, with this type of mentality you no longer have any desire to live holy, go to church, listen to God, turn to Him, pray, or seek salvation, even on your deathbed. "And even as they did not like to retain God in their knowledge, God gave them over to a reprobate mind, to do those things which are not convenient" (Romans 1:28 KJV).

Committing spiritual suicide can be an unusually prolonged process. It doesn't happen overnight. We commit spiritual suicide when we reject the life Jesus gave us through His death, burial, and resurrection. It happens when we carry anger, resentment, prejudice, hate, and other such emotions that can destroy our spirit over time.

Our spirit belongs to the Lord. He can repossess it anytime He wants. Yes, our spirit is eternal because it's of the Lord, but He can withdraw His Holy Spirit from us and we can remain alive. God does this by inhaling the breath that He exhaled, which gave us life (see Genesis 2:7). Though God will never leave you, He may begin distancing His presence from you when you are unsaved, the longer you refuse to conform to His will.

No individual can come to the Lord Jesus Christ unless God orchestrates it. Jesus told us, "No one can come to Me unless the Father who sent Me draws him; and I will raise him up at the last day" (John 6:44). He also told us, "I am the way, the truth, and the life. No one can come to the Father except through Me" (John 14:6 NLT). No one can even get to the Father except by the Son. Guess what: Obedience can and will bring you closer.

Obedience Is a Weapon

Obedience is key to combatting spiritual suicide; it is your weapon against hell. In fact, if you're willing and obedient, you will eat the good of the land (see Isaiah 1:19).

When you eat spiritual things—fasting, praying in tongues, worshiping, and reading and obeying God's Word—you will get *fat* in the spirit. Isaiah 10:27 (AMPC) makes reference to yokes (bondage or restrictions) being "destroyed because of fatness." That fatness equates to spiritual healthiness. You will not and cannot die spiritually when you maintain this type of diet.

As you are feasting, set your ears to hear and obey everything the Lord has instructed you to do. This is crucial. The Lord will give you the grace to do what He has commanded.

> For the grace of God that brings salvation has appeared to all men, teaching us that, denying ungodliness and worldly lusts, we should live soberly, righteously, and godly in the present age.
>
> Titus 2:11–12

YOUR BATTLE PLAN

Fast and pray for a spiritual detox, cut ungodly soul ties, protect your hearing, be careful of your environment, and walk in obedience, holiness, and righteousness as never before. Read the Bible aloud daily. When evil thoughts invade your mind, immediately cast them out in Jesus' name. Afterward, I want you to repeat out loud (and commit to memory) the following Scripture:

> Finally, brethren, whatever things are true, whatever things are noble, whatever things are just, whatever things are pure, whatever things are lovely, whatever things are of good report, if there

is any virtue and if there is anything praiseworthy—meditate on these things.

Philippians 4:8

Also, saturate your environment with the sounds of heaven. You can do this by playing anointed Christian music, listening to a Spirit-filled leader, or playing an audio version of the Bible in your home or automobile. The sound doesn't have to be loud. Demons can hear it even at the lowest levels. They've been tormenting you, so now it's your turn to torment them.

YOUR BATTLE PRAYER

Father, in the name of Jesus, don't let me be spiritually dead and not even realize it. Lord, I thank you that I am alive in you. I come against spiritual suicide and every demonic entity behind it. These spirits will not come near me or my family. I rebuke every demon that attempts to initiate my spiritual death. I will not experience a premature spiritual death. Glory!

Lord, I refuse to walk in rebellion against you to the point that you begin to withdraw your presence from me. Rebellion will have no place in me. I thank you for all the second, third, and fourth chances you have given me. Even when I was walking according to my own will, not yours, you loved me enough to correct me. Proverbs 3:12 (NLT) tells me this about you: "For the LORD corrects those he loves, just as a father corrects a child in whom he delights." Father, I am so honored to be your child.

Obedience is your love language, Lord. You are pleased by faith, according to Hebrews 11:6. Father, I will fast regularly. I will pray daily. I will read the Bible aloud. I will go on a spiritual detox to get anything that is not of you out of me. Show me any ungodly soul ties, and I will cut them. Lord, I will watch over my ear gates and eye gates, not allowing anything that's not of you to enter. Let my obedience to you be my weapon against the devil. Lord, I thank you that you always hear me when I pray. Praise your holy name. Amen!

(Note: Your praise is a weapon. Begin praising the Lord now, right where you are, to seal this prayer.)

Ego and Chasing Celebrity Status

For people will love only themselves and their money. They will be boastful and proud, scoffing at God, disobedient to their parents, and ungrateful. They will consider nothing sacred. They will be unloving and unforgiving; they will slander others and have no self-control. They will be cruel and hate what is good. They will betray their friends, be reckless, be puffed up with pride, and love pleasure rather than God. They will act religious, but they will reject the power that could make them godly. Stay away from people like that!

—2 Timothy 3:2–5 NLT

One of the traps that Satan uses is a celebrity mentality because so many people, both in and out of the Church, want it. A *spirit of celebrity* has been slowly creeping into the Church for years, and now it's here.

Don't get me wrong—celebrity status can be used for good if it promotes the agenda of Jesus Christ and His Gospel.

Unfortunately, the devil often uses it to get us to shift the focus from the Lord to ourselves. The *Cambridge Dictionary* defines *ego* as "your idea or opinion of yourself, especially your feeling of your own importance and ability."[1] In Greek, *ego* translates as "I am" or "I exist." Dictionary.com defines it as "the 'I' or self of any person."[2] Ego is the identical twin of pride and the cousin of the spirit of celebrity.

Self, self-image, self-worth, and self-esteem, when linked to ego and pride, are also part of this demon's family. Did you notice that *self* is quite prominent in this unholy household? Please keep that in mind. When someone is egotistical, all that matters is self. This self-centeredness can also be a demonic spirit, desiring worship, glorification, adulation, credit, and acknowledgment. When a *spirit of self-centeredness* is present, the spirit called celebrity comes in and wants to take over. A person's ego is the vehicle, and notoriety, the fuel.

In his book *Celebrity*, Professor Chris Rojek states, "Although God-like qualities are often attributed to celebrities, the modern meaning of the term *celebrity* actually derives from the fall of the gods, and the rise of democratic governments and secular societies."[3] Unfortunately, many celebrities are viewed as gods because of their notoriety, public exposure, and popularity. Anyone can be a celebrity these days, especially with the advent of social media. This can create an atmosphere that is conducive to idol worship. Rojek adds, "Celebrity worship is regularly condemned in public as idolatry, which carries connotations of slavery, false consciousness and the 'Devil's work.'"[4]

The enemy specializes in offering material things in exchange for spiritual admission into your life. He offered Jesus "all the kingdoms of the world and their splendor" (Matthew 4:8 NIV). Satan had the power to give Jesus these because of mankind's fall in the Garden of Eden, but that's another story. He still makes this kind of offer today. Sadly, quite a few people have accepted his "new deal," their very souls being the currency.

The Bible asks us two pertinent questions: (1) What does it profit a person to gain the whole world and lose his or her soul? (2) What can someone give in exchange for his or her soul? (see Mark 8:36–37). People can sell their souls without realizing it. They do this by making gods out of whomever or whatever they idolize. Behind each idol someone puts before the Lord resides a demon (see Deuteronomy 32:16–17).

Some worldly celebrities today have made it very clear whom and what they worship. They have become dreadfully obvious in their adoration of Satan, yet some Christians continue to listen to their music, watch their videos, and even attend their concerts. These celebrities will occasionally come out with some so-called "Christian content" to deceive you into believing that they're godly, but ultimately, it's all smoke and mirrors. Don't be deceived.

Status Chasers vs. God Chasers

Satan's strategy is to get the saints to become status chasers instead of God chasers. Social media status is quickly becoming the measure of godliness among Christians. If you don't have a huge following, you're considered less anointed than someone who does. This has created a desire in people to prove themselves by increasing their presence online, basically chasing their status among people instead of improving their status with God.

This is what Satan wants. Regrettably, his plan seems to be working. Many are chasing celebrity status in lieu of chasing the Lord, preferring the praise of people over the approval of the Father (see Matthew 10:28). They've allowed the fear of others' opinions to dominate their fear of (reverence for) God. The enemy uses the fear of mankind as a tactic to trap us, but when we place our trust in the Lord, there is safety (see Proverbs 29:25).

A demonic *spirit of selfish ambition* is hurting the Church. This is not the ministry of Christ. We must always be on guard against this self-destructive spirit (see James 3:14–16). It can infect anyone, including me. Many start off with right, godly intentions, but some, when they get a taste of fame in ministry or life, forget their initial motivation for answering the call of God. This demon's scheme is to get them to forget.

Numerous people are so enamored by the celebrity of ministry that they ignore its selfless aspect. They look at the money, clothes, homes, television appearances, books, etc., rather than the pure joy that comes with just loving the Father. The spirit behind this attack implements its plan slowly and steadily. This starts with getting people to think it's all about them (ego), above the call of God on their lives. This demon has led many well-intended men and women astray.

Signs that this spirit has infiltrated individuals are evidenced in their speech, behavior, and actions. Like Lucifer before his fall from heaven, their focus is mainly on themselves, not God. In a group, people infected by selfishness must dominate the dialogue by being exceedingly verbose (talkative), hearing others but not really listening. Selfishness, which finds its origin within the Satanic kingdom, infiltrates their writing, thoughts, and conversation. Be on the lookout for this cunning spirit. It has led many down the wrong path.

A Transparent Moment

My reasons for getting into ministry were never for celebrity status or platforms. Can I be transparent for a moment? I went into it kicking and screaming. I didn't want to be a preacher, pastor, or prophet. To be completely honest, I didn't come from a family that frequented church. I hated going to church as a kid. I was raised Roman Catholic. When God called me, I asked Him to confirm it so often that He got upset by the frequency of my requests. I finally answered His call on my life, and it hasn't been the same since. It has been a wonderful, yet perilous journey thus far.

Fame should never be your primary goal when getting into ministry. Your aspiration shouldn't be to become the Beyoncé or Jay-Z of Christendom. The goal should be to serve Jesus Christ, our famous Lord. Along with a *spirit of selfish ambition* and a *spirit of arrogance*, a *spirit of fame* has hit the Church today. This bothers me. Some in the Body of Christ have equated the fivefold ministry with worldly popularity, not realizing that the ministry gifts are given for the purpose of servanthood. Jesus told us that the world loves its own, but when you're not of the world, it will hate you. This is why others may detest you. The more you look, speak, and act like Jesus, the more you'll be hated (see John 15:18–19).

Regrettably, some of that malice comes from inside the Church. Just because someone regularly attends the house of the Lord doesn't mean he or she is a partaker of His salvation. There are those who pursue fivefold ministry to procure an advantage over a peer, a congregation, or, believe it or not, a social media page. This is never a good reason to become an apostle, prophet, evangelist, pastor, or teacher. Ministry should never be only about individual success.

We are admonished in Scripture to esteem others better than ourselves, but how often does that really happen?

Let nothing be done through selfish ambition or conceit, but in lowliness of mind *let each esteem others better than himself.* Let each of you look out not only for his own interests, but also for the interests of others. Let this mind be in you which was also in Christ Jesus.

Philippians 2:3–5, emphasis added

Disappointingly, the opposite of these verses is true as well. *Spirits of arrogance, competition, jealousy,* and *backbiting* have infiltrated a lot of ministries. It's absolutely heartbreaking. We debate, argue, slander, fight, and gossip like never before. As the Body of Christ, we should find ourselves in positions of humility, praying for each other instead of preying on each other. Some people need to get over themselves and get into God so that they can successfully do His will.

Could I get closer to God? Absolutely. Could I hear from Him better? Definitely. Am I perfect? Not even close! Like you, I'm a work in progress. I'm nowhere near being complete. I love God and His people, but they're hard to deal with at times, as am I. These days, I'm primarily working on being delivered from the thoughts and opinions of others. I'm learning not to let callous, unprovoked attacks bother me. I'm slowly but surely making great strides. You'll be in a good place once you get delivered from demons and the people who love them.

Godly Leadership or Fallen Celebrities?

As some of our more famous religious leaders continue in sin, why do we support them? Are we drawn in by their celebrity status, or by the anointing? To continue following fallen leaders is indicative of endorsing their chronic wrongdoing. I'm not referring to a leader falling once or twice and repenting. I'm talking about repeated indiscretions like sexual perversion, adultery, pedophilia, sex out of wedlock, etc.

I, for one, am tired of hearing that we should *only* pray for such leaders. What about holding these individuals accountable by withholding our patronage in the form of our time, ability, and finances? I bet they'd be quick to change for the better then. Money talks. It has a language. According to Ecclesiastes 10:19, it has an answer for everything. We shouldn't continue to back fallen leaders based on an unnatural love for their names instead of the One who created them. Some church leaders openly support these fallen folks when they know they're wrong. This is possibly because of the church leader's attachment to the celebrity minister's sphere of influence. These leaders do not want to lose the influence, wealth, and prestige that come with their connection to the fallen leader. This is why most won't leave them.

I yearn to see more godly leaders who desire God's face more than His hand. Who want souls won more than they want their name in lights. Whose passion is to continue to make Jesus famous, over being "social media famous" themselves. Such Christian leaders want God's glory above their own. They refuse to let money prevent them from preaching the Gospel. They are not too big to preach at a church with a small congregation. I could go on, but I won't. Please pray for more of these types of leaders, because we sorely need them today.

Also, please examine the lives (including the integrity, character, and personal history) of the leaders you submit to. Some believers have unintentionally placed themselves under leadership currently involved in deep sin. We should consult the Lord first when submitting ourselves or our ministries to a particular person or entity. Our decision should not be based on a leader's popularity, platform, or positioning.

If a leader's relationship with you is based only on the money you sow into him or her, then you don't have a true relationship with that overseer at all. What happens to the relationship if you're unable to sow or give huge amounts of money anymore? Does it change? If it does, it wasn't godly, but fleshly. Keep in mind that the anointing (oil) flows from the top down (see Psalm 133:2). Whatever is in the head will be in the body. In other words, whatever is in a leader, good or bad, will eventually get on you.

The Spirit of Competition

Recently, I was invited to minister at a good friend's anniversary service. Another minister was also on the roster to speak. I was given an allotted time to deliver an encouraging word to the pastor and congregants. I preached what was in my spirit with fire, anointing, and zeal within the time given, as instructed.

The prophet after me asked the crowd, "How can I follow that?" I initially took that to mean he enjoyed my message—until his preaching began. With eyes popping out and a contorted face, this guest minister hollered, sweated, spit, twirled, and darted from one side of the altar to the other. He went way over the time the host gave him. As I watched in total disbelief, I realized that this person, my co-laborer in the Gospel, was competing with me. The Bible calls such competition ignorant:

> Oh, don't worry; we wouldn't dare say that we are as wonderful as these other men who tell you how important they are! But they are only comparing themselves with each other, using themselves as the standard of measurement. How ignorant!
>
> 2 Corinthians 10:12 NLT

I was speaking to my great friend and colleague, Apostle Nona McKenzie Parker, sometime later, and she told me that when people start looking at you *competitively*, they stop looking at you *compassionately*. Truer words have never been spoken. Don't allow competition or jealousy to rise up in you when it comes to the blessings of God on the lives of others. Celebrity, greed, envy, and idolatry have permeated the Church. These spirits must be called out and cast out because they are the instigators of competition. The Bible tells us instead, "Rejoice with those who rejoice" (Romans 12:15).

If you're competing with your brother or sister in Christ, you're not in the will of the Lord. I've seen this over and over again, and it's discouraging. This is not a competition, but it is a race (see 1 Corinthians 9:24). We are running it to make heaven, but we shouldn't trample each other in the process. There's nothing wrong with leaving a godly legacy, but there's something wrong with purposely wounding others to do it.

One should never look at the blessings of other believers and wonder why they were blessed, or whether or not they deserved that door of extraordinary opportunity. We shouldn't think, *I'm more anointed! That door was meant for me, not them!* This behavior typifies an unsaved or unregenerated mentality. The Bible is very clear about how the Lord feels when we compare ourselves with one another. As you can see from another translation of 2 Corinthians 10:12, the New King James Version, it's clearly unwise: "For we dare not class ourselves or compare ourselves with those who commend themselves. But they, measuring themselves by themselves, and comparing themselves among themselves, are not wise."

Competition in Marriages

On more than one occasion, I have witnessed husbands competing with their wives, and vice versa. This should not be. When this occurs, the spouses are competing with themselves, because when a man and a woman marry, they become one flesh (see Genesis 2:24).

In a marital competition, the offending partner allows the *spirit of jealousy* to create friction in the marriage. *Ahab and Jezebel spirits* are in operation here as well. Let's focus on celebrating each other's accomplishments instead, especially if it's our spouse. To do otherwise does not exemplify the love of the Father, but does encourage the operations of Satan.

The *spirit of competition* is alive and well, walking today's earthly realm. Let's kill it by showing one another our genuine support and love. Share your spouse's accomplishments on your social media page. You can also email your spouse a note so that some encouragement is waiting in his or her inbox. You can text your spouse congratulations for an accomplishment, call him or her, or just say it in person.

If people think they're too big to do this for their marriage partner, they've already been infected by the spirit of competition. Some people who are contaminated by this spirit don't even realize it. The Bible advises, "Let us not become conceited, or provoke one another, or be jealous of one another" (Galatians 5:26 NLT). We would do well to take heed of these words.

Your Buddy Named *Humble*

God promoted Saul when he was humble. But pride grew and exposed itself, causing him to be stripped of the kingdom and the Lord's presence. Some leaders who receive promotion from the Lord start off very much like King Saul, little in their own sight (see 1 Samuel 15:17). Yet once recognition, fame, and money come, humility gets kicked out of their lives.

When the Lord is truly the head of your life, self-importance cannot grow and spread. Instead, the more He is in your life, the more love, mercy, honor, and integrity will be present. The closer you are to God, the meeker you should become, because our Lord exudes humility (see Philippians 2:8).

The desire to serve should override any desire for celebrity. The more that we humble ourselves and serve, the more God will exalt us in due time. Don't fall out with your buddy named *humble*. Remember, it cost Saul the kingdom. "Humble yourselves therefore under the mighty hand of God, that he may exalt you in due time" (1 Peter 5:6 KJV).

In the days to come, however, some generals of the faith will be replaced because of pride, rebellion, mismanagement, and mishandling of the Lord's people. Others will be demoted because of secret sins that will be exposed. The Lord is no longer promoting the arrogant while humility is absent. In fact, He is demoting arrogant leaders until humility returns.

The Spirit of Character Assassination

Along with leaders chasing celebrity status, the *spirit of character assassination* is at an all-time high in the land. It gets its strength from jealousy, rejection, and insecurity. We can defeat this spirit by not *killing* the names of other people behind closed doors through our texts, emails, or phone calls.

If someone continues to slam others when speaking to you, shut it down. You can do this by ending the conversation or simply changing the subject. You don't need that messiness in your spirit. Don't let people dump verbal trash on you. You're not a garbage can!

Because of this spirit of character assassination, you can form a preconceived notion about another person without ever meeting him or her. Please find out the truth about others for yourself. There is way too much slander in the Body of Christ that is based on someone else's personal opinions (see Psalm 101:5). Get to know a targeted person for yourself, and then make an informed decision about his or her character. If you've heard that he or she did something crazy, go and ask that person directly instead of asking everyone else (see Exodus 20:16).

When we assassinate the character of others, we're actually doing the devil's job for him (see Proverbs 16:28). The Lord frowns on such conduct: "Do not speak evil of one another, brethren. He who speaks evil of a brother and judges his brother, speaks evil of the law and judges the law. But if you judge the law, you are not a doer of the law but a judge" (James 4:11).

Platforms Are Replacing Altars

We should never slander or murder the names (reputations) of other leaders or saints simply because we don't like them. Repeating unproven accusations to anyone is an ungodly move. If ministry leaders tell others that they won't participate as a conference speaker unless one of the guests they don't care for is removed, what message are they sending? That behavior is more *diva* than *divine* and smacks of ego. This exemplifies the mind of a celebrity rather than the mind of Christ. Sure, this is commonplace in the world, but it shouldn't be in the Church.

Such individuals demean those they don't care for behind closed doors. They're not man or woman enough to address the person directly, but like snakes, they do it low to the ground, where they can't be seen easily. Individuals of this ilk will preach against such cowardly actions, but alas, will be its biggest perpetrators. This is hypocrisy at its finest.

When anyone intentionally goes out of his or her way to malign the character of godly people, judgment will be that person's portion. Such people will reap what they've sown (see Galatians 6:7). It bothers me that this kind of talk has gained much ground within the Body of Christ these days. "But I say to you that for every idle word men may speak, they will give account of it in the day of judgment" (Matthew 12:36).

Celebrity has clearly begun to outweigh servanthood in these circles. *Platforms are quickly replacing altars.*

If a person's main goal in ministry is to become a celebrity, he or she should get out. We must all seek God's face and righteousness before we seek His platform. When we do this, we will gain access to His stage (see Matthew 6:33). We must yield our platforms to Him. Our focus and energy should be on Jesus Christ, not the downfall of others. Be careful of those who insincerely smile in your face, then assassinate your character behind your back. Sadly, it happens more frequently than you might imagine. Become like the psalmist who wrote, "Whoever slanders their neighbor in secret, I will put to silence; whoever has haughty eyes and a proud heart, I will not tolerate" (Psalm 101:5 NIV).

"You Have to Play the Game"

In certain circles, I've heard ministry referred to as a game. Those in these same circles have advised others to "play the game." Since when did winning souls become a game? How can the Gospel itself be called a game? Here are twelve rules that insincere game players put into practice:

Twelve Characteristics of the Game

1. Only preach feel-good messages instead of life-changing, corrective ones.
2. Celebrity, instead of God, is lord.
3. Pretend to like people just because of their influence.
4. Omit any references to sin in messages, because it will kill the offering.
5. Align yourself with popular groups solely to augment your personal platform.
6. Ostracize others just because they don't agree with you.
7. Formulate a plan to indoctrinate others into your network instead of the Lord's army.
8. Attach yourself to whoever's hot right now.
9. Don't step on any toes.
10. You're blacklisted if you refuse to play the game.
11. No desire to reach the lost.
12. Always remember the rules of the game.

Servanthood over Celebrity

Self-promotion is not God's promotion. Too many times, preachers think in terms of celebrity, not servanthood. They'll inbox you on social media platforms, angling for an engagement that's not about mission or ministry, but monetary gain. They should allow the Lord to open ministerial doors so they won't have to use gimmicks, gifting, or manipulation to open their own doors. If they allow it, God will open doors for them that no man can shut (see Revelation 3:8).

Never be too big to do the little things, or too little to do the big things. Humility is the key to greatness in God.

If you value a name over an anointing, you'll be disappointed every time. Neither celebrity nor carnal success equates to being a servant of God. No matter how much God elevates you, *stay humble!* Remember, it's about servanthood, not celebrity. I'm praying that one day, servanthood will usurp celebrity within the church world.

A boldness is coming upon the Body of Christ, especially among prophetic people. Authentic voices are arising that won't be bought by platforms, celebrities, or finances. The celebrity leader mindset must be replaced by a servant leader mindset. Arrogance has no place in the pulpit. Look at the following symptoms of placing celebrity over servanthood. If you have at least four of the following twelve signs, then you've probably been infected by the spirit of celebrity. (Note: Some of the signs below are satirical, yet serious.)

Twelve Signs of Acting Like a Celebrity, Not a Servant

1. You're drawn to carnal instead of spiritual things.
2. Carnal things begin to dominate spiritual things in your life.
3. It becomes easier and easier to sin even though you're saved.
4. You actually believe your own hype.
5. It's more about you than your God-given mandate.
6. When people praise you, you don't redirect their adoration to God.
7. Mammon (wealth) takes the place of your mantle (mission).
8. Your prayer life is at an all-time low.
9. When you enter the church, everyone must stand.

10. You consistently evoke your title when someone speaks to you.

11. You're afraid to like a colleague's social media post because you think it may give the person a leg up over you.

12. The majority of the pictures you post on social media are selfies or videos of you walking in slow motion. (I'm joking. Sort of.)

Choosing celebrity over servanthood is serious business spiritually. I sense the Lord giving me an urgent prophetic warning to share here: *Ministries will be dismantled that are headed by leaders who have consistently mishandled the Lord's sheep. They have ignored His many warnings and live a life behind closed doors that does not reflect the holiness of His presence. Like Saul, some who have been mean-spirited, miserly, selfish, greedy, and haughty will decline in regard to their influence, popularity, and following. Their numbers will decrease as the Lord moves His sheep to greener pastures. The Lord will not share His glory with anyone. The opportunistic spirit that has infiltrated churches will be discerned and addressed. True shepherds will replace the false ones who have allowed mammon to become their lord. Many who considered godliness only for gain will be identified, and what was gathered by deception will be dispersed to those with the greatest need. The celebrity spirit in the Church must die, and platforms must be given back to the Lord. In the not too distant future, the fear of the Lord will return to the earth.*

The Greatest Leaders Are *Humble*

The most outstanding leaders I've ever seen in the Body of Christ usually share the trait of humility. They don't allow pride to infuse their being based on the enormity of their congregations, social media following, or churches they're covering.

These kinds of leaders are rare. They're sold out to Jesus, not their egos. They're not concerned with personal celebrity, only with making the name of Jesus more known. It's never about them, but about Him. I'm not talking about false humility, but true soberness in the spirit.

When you see pride in a leader, pray. Pride caused Lucifer's fall from heaven (see Isaiah 14:12–14). We must all guard against the *spirit of pride*. Pride and falling are interconnected, and pride always precedes a fall (see Proverbs 16:18).

Always be on guard against this spirit. It has a tendency to sneak up on you. One of the signs that you have pride is when you deny it, because everyone deals with it on some level. It is always lingering or nearby, just waiting for an opportunity to get in. Disappointingly, many a great ministry leader has fallen due to pride. This spirit truly should not be found among the saints of God. There is nothing wrong with thinking highly of yourself, but not too highly. As Paul wrote, "For I say, through the grace given to me, to everyone who is among you, not to think of himself more highly than he ought to think, but to think soberly, as God has dealt to each one a measure of faith" (Romans 12:3).

Stay *humble*, and the Lord will exalt you. As He elevates you, make sure humility is your constant companion.

If you're a church leader, use your weight wisely. When gaining influence or "weight" in the spirit and the natural, never use it to attack people who have left your church or ministry. That smacks of rejection, anger, bitterness, and offense. Every relationship should include the fruit of the Spirit—love, joy, peace, long-suffering, gentleness, goodness, faith, meekness, and temperance (see Galatians 5:22–23 KJV). If it doesn't, it's not of God.

Why do some feel the need to tear down other people or assassinate their character just because they've left a particular ministry? Some will slander their names through stinging social media posts. This behavior is more like the spirit of Saul than David. The Lord is not pleased with this. Those who are doing this will reap what they have sown, and the reaping is almost always more significant than the sowing. Use your spiritual weight wisely.

I just heard this in my spirit and sense the Lord saying to us,

Be careful whom you align with. You're sometimes known by the company you keep. Pray about alignments and wait to see if they're divine. If not, keep moving. Misalignment, the incorrect arrangement or position of something in relation to something else, can cost you. "For everything that is hidden will eventually be brought into the open, and every secret will be brought to light" [Mark 4:22 NLT].

The Trap of Celebrity Parents

"Spiritual parenting" can be an incredible experience, if you have the right spiritual parents—meaning those who are supplied by the Lord. In reference to the now defunct popular television program *The Maury Povich Show*, many men were thought to be the father of a certain child (or children), but DNA evidence would often prove otherwise. Maury would frequently rely on DNA testing to prove or disprove family relationships. Your spiritual DNA should match your spiritual parents. In some cases, it doesn't match. When it doesn't, the results indicate that he or she is not your father or mother.

You should never choose a spiritual parent based on his or her level of celebrity or notoriety. This is a huge mistake. Such a choice clearly shows a heart and motive issue on your part. This decision was probably birthed from the hope of gaining access to the person's platform and power, rather than as confirmation of a God-ordained connection.

When I think of proper fatherhood in the spirit, I think of Paul and Timothy. I routinely use them as models. Paul called Timothy his son in several Scriptures (see 1 Corinthians 4:17;

1 Timothy 1:2, 18; 2 Timothy 1:2; 2:1). In fact, Paul had other spiritual sons as well, Onesimus and Titus (see Philemon 1:10; Titus 1:4). In addition, he had many more than these (as evidenced in 1 Corinthians 4:14–15). Here, let's focus on Timothy. He was raised by his grandmother (Lois) and mother (Eunice), according to 2 Timothy 1:5. Scripture doesn't mention a biological father, so he needed a spiritual father to fill that void. He found one in Paul.

A month before my natural mother died suddenly, Ruth Brown became my spiritual mother. God chose her for me, and I said yes. Though the Lord chose her, I still had to consent. She never hinted at becoming my spiritual mother. I just followed the leading of the Holy Spirit. That's paramount in whom you allow to be your spiritual parent.

There are those who want to be somebody's spiritual parent. I don't agree, however, with seeking that position in the lives of others. I cover (oversee) or mentor a number of people. Never once did I pursue them or suggest that I needed to be their "daddy in the spirit." Yet some do this as a form of gaining control over others. For example, it's harder for a spiritual son or daughter to leave a church than it is if they are simply members.

When someone is pressuring you to be his or her spiritual son or daughter, that's usually an indication that the person is not your spiritual parent. God will show you who should be a parent to you. Until then, and even afterward, the Lord is your primary covering. There is no time as a believer that you are uncovered. Don't let anyone manipulate you into thinking you must have a spiritual daddy or mommy to make it in ministry. Are spiritual parents a benefit? Unquestionably. But forced spiritual parenthood is not godly; it's abusive.

Some might say that you can't choose your parents. That's so true in the natural, but not so much in the spiritual. Yes, God can and will show you who your spiritual parents are, but it's up to you to say yes or no. Free will is still in effect in today's world.

The Rise of Authentic Leaders

Many of the uncalled who occupy pulpits meant for the called are being exposed in this hour. I was in prayer recently when I heard this in my spirit: *Exposure is not coming—it's already here!* Leaders today who have hidden sin in their lives are being exposed at an alarming speed. The covers are literally being pulled off with supernatural acceleration. Some of these people are friends of mine. While I'm praying for them, I know this is the Lord's doing. It must be this way so that the new guard can replace the old one. These individuals who make up the old guard are being replaced by authentic people who are not obsessed with worldly celebrity status. For the new guard, it will be more important to celebrate the birth of Christ publicly instead of their own birthdays.

While I was in prayer, the Lord also emphasized to me the importance of a good name. Proverbs 22:1 states, "A good name is to be chosen rather than great riches, loving favor rather than silver and gold." Authentic leaders' names (reputations) will carry weight due to their adherence to keeping their names in good standing. In fact, their names will carry more spiritual weight than their titles or offices within the fivefold ministry.

These authentic leaders will have the heart of God concerning His people, instead of a heart that desires mammon (wealth) more. They will train and not disdain the equipping of the sheep. They will spend sufficient time activating, educating, and equipping potential leaders for ministry, instead of making them wait many years before starting their churches. They will thrust other leaders into ministry, instead of making empty promises without ever intending to send them out. Humility will be their hallmark. Arrogance will be foreign to them. Any consistent conceit you see in a current leader will be your sign to begin planning your exodus because a plague is on its way. Humble leaders will consistently utilize godly platforms to help other struggling, authentic, emerging ones.

While a remnant of leaders today has not bowed to Baal, a good number who have remains. From them we get astronomical registration fees, outrageous offerings taken up that they themselves would never give, unreasonable speaking requests, false prophecies rooted in greed, controlling churches, a stifling of independent prophetic thoughts and actions, no true deliverance, carnal conferences with no real power, so-called invisible miracles, and, most regrettably, no true love for God's people. Instead of gravitating to the latest ministerial fad, look for genuine churches led by untainted leaders. Go to churches where leaders encourage you to do the works of the Kingdom, not just sit in the pews.

YOUR BATTLE PLAN

Fast to break the spirit of pride. Submit yourself to God daily, hourly, moment by moment. Break all ungodly soul ties with carnally motivated people, and curate godly relationships with like-minded people who go after substance, contentment, stewardship, and Kingdom prosperity. I highly recommend reading the following battle prayer aloud daily, until you feel the spirits of pride, celebrity, ego, and the like lift off you. Each time that you pray, seal it with enthusiastic and authentic praise to the Lord!

YOUR BATTLE PRAYER

Father God, in the name of Jesus, I come against the spirits of competition, comparison, and celebrity that have crept into the Church and social media. Hell has designed these spirits to derail, deny, divide, and ultimately destroy me. I bind the plans of these spirits. I thwart their genesis and abort their future in my life. I reject and renounce all demonic platforms, replacing each of them with godly altars full of fire, glory, and love. Lord, I give my platform back to you. Do with it what you will, because I trust you with everything I own. You are a good Father who has equipped me with eyes to see and ears to hear the tactics of the enemies of my soul.

God, show me any evidence of ego in me, and I will cast it out in the name of Jesus. When I read your Word, let it be like a mirror to my soul, allowing me to see everything in me that's not like you, so I can cast it out. As 2 Timothy 3:2–5 instructs, I will not be a lover of money, boastful, and proud. I will not scoff at you, Lord, and be ungrateful. I will not slander others, lacking in the self-control of my mouth. I refuse to betray friends, be reckless, be puffed up with pride, and love pleasure rather than you, God. In fact, I will avoid people like that unless I'm witnessing to them about my Savior and Lord, Jesus Christ.

Thank you, Father, for opening my eyes regarding chasing celebrity status and self-centeredness. Let my thoughts, conversations, and actions be always centered around you. Please strengthen me to choose servanthood over celebrity status every time. Don't allow me to give in to my ego. I don't want to play any games when it comes to the seriousness of your call on my life, and ministering to and serving your people. I will be a God chaser instead of a celebrity chaser. I come against the spirit of character assassination that may have been a result of past ungodly associations. I reject misalignments regarding my relationships with others, and I call forth alignment with the people whom you have already chosen to walk with me. Lord, I love you, and I appreciate that you always hear me. Thank you!

(Note: Begin praising the Lord now, right where you are, to seal this prayer.)

The Demon of Distraction

Let your eyes look directly forward, and your gaze be
straight before you. Ponder the path of your feet; then all
your ways will be sure. Do not swerve to the right or to the
left; turn your foot away from evil.

—Proverbs 4:25–27 ESV

The *demon of distraction* and his associates are malevolent spirits
straight from the pit of hell that are assigned to sidetrack, divert,
disturb, and befuddle you so that you don't embark on or finish
what the Lord has assigned you to do. Instead of being destiny
assistants like the angels, they are inherently destiny inhibitors
assigned to us by the evil one. They routinely disguise themselves
as blessings, but they're actually stumbling blocks designed to
stop you from achieving what the Lord has clearly told you that
you could do. The *King James Bible Dictionary* defines *distraction* as "confusion from a multiplicity of objects *crowding on the
mind* and calling the attention different ways; perturbation of
mind; perplexity . . . [See 1 Corinthians 7:35]" (emphasis added;
brackets in original).[1] In addition, it is "the act of distracting; a
drawing apart; separation."[2]

These malevolent spirits want to pull you out of the will of God. As I talked about in chapter 3, the assault by these demonic entities begins in the mind, with the goal that whatever dominates you mentally will eventually be acted out in the flesh. As I previously mentioned, you will become what you think on the most. Satan is counting on this.

Have you ever made up your mind to read the Bible every night before going to bed, only to find yourself drifting off to sleep after reading only a chapter or two? Did you ever promise God that you were going to fast the next day, only to be confronted by your favorite foods at work and give in to temptation? Have you ever walked out to your car to go to church on Sunday morning and found a flat tire? All these distractions and more are endorsed by hell. It's laughable, but true. The enemy has a tendency to stage the greatest distraction of your life when the Lord is about to open the greatest door of your life.

Tempted by a Distraction

I want to be very transparent here. Years ago, I was presented with something that appealed to my flesh, but not my spirit. A common tactic the devil uses is to appeal to our carnal nature. He does this by providing the type of temptation that he knows will draw you. For example, if you were bound by alcohol, he's not going to tempt you with cigarettes. It could be material objects instead, or success, or money, or the opposite sex (which I will delve into later in this chapter). Your spirit wants to do the God thing, but many times your flesh will war against your spirit. Sometimes carnality wins, but you can't let it.

I prayed about what was facing me and even confided in close friends. It was one of my toughest challenges as a man of God. I had to do as Jesus told His disciples in Matthew 26:41: "Watch and pray, lest you enter into temptation. The spirit indeed is willing, but the flesh is weak."

One of the friends I entrusted with what I was going through revealed it to my wife under the guise of a prophetic word. All hell broke loose when I saw Elisa that evening. Now, to ease your mind, I did not have an affair. I have been faithful to my wife, to whom I've been married for almost thirty years. Without going into too much detail, however, intrinsically I knew that if I gave in to this distraction, I would abort the great things God had in store for me. Has such a thing ever happened to you? You have no idea what you will do until you're in the midst of the temptation. When you are on the verge of an unprecedented breakthrough, the enemy's tactic is to intensify your distractions. His goal is to get you to do irreparable damage to your reputation, marriage, and ministry.

Earlier that same year, the Lord had shown me that it was time to prepare for travel, referring to itinerant ministry. He had tremendous blessings on the horizon. The devil presented something that could have nullified all of this, as well as potentially end or severely damage my public ministry. Thankfully, I had enough discernment, wisdom, and foresight not to allow myself to get sidetracked. I was being tested, and I passed and continued with the Lord's directives for my life. If I had given in to this major diversion, you probably wouldn't be reading this book right now. So many ministerial opportunities presented themselves to me after that test. Praise God that I stayed the course—and you can, too!

This is exactly what evil spirits will do with you. When you're on the verge of something divinely phenomenal, a demon of distraction will show up to upset it. You may be in a similar situation at this moment. Hold on to the unchanging hand of God, and He won't let you be swayed by the devil's tactics. Resist the devil, and he will run away from you (see James 4:7).

The Author of Most Distractions

If God is not the author of confusion, then the devil is (see 1 Corinthians 14:33). Not only is Satan the author of confusion; he is also the author of most distractions. In the Garden of Eden, Adam and Eve were sidetracked by the snake's subtlety and words, which mixed a bit of the truth with lies (see Genesis 3:1). Because of this, Eve gave in to temptation and ate the fruit from the Tree of Knowledge of Good and Evil, which God had strictly forbidden (see Genesis 2:16–17). She presented the fruit to her husband, and he ate it as well, causing the fall of all mankind.

The serpent played upon what both Adam and Eve had probably desired for a while. The snake possibly had been observing them for quite some time, planning his attack and sensing their mutual desire and curiosity. This is an innate part of us—to want what we're denied. The enemy knew this and played upon it. He cannot tempt you with something that's not attractive to you. In order to distract you, there must be some level of attraction. "Stolen waters are sweet, and bread eaten in secret is pleasant" (Proverbs 9:17 KJV).

The temptation was meant to pull Eve's focus off God's instructions and onto the desires of her flesh. Once that lust was cultivated, Lucifer could initiate his plan so that both she and her husband did something contrary to the Lord's instructions. The devil knew that if he could persuade the woman first, the man would follow because he trusted her. Why? Because she was part of him. In essence, she was he, as these verses show:

> And the rib, which the LORD God had taken from man, made he a woman, and brought her unto the man.
> And Adam said, This is now bone of my bones, and flesh of my flesh: she shall be called Woman, because she was taken out of Man.
> Therefore shall a man leave his father and his mother, and shall cleave unto his wife: and they shall be one flesh.
>
> Genesis 2:22–24 KJV

Adam and Eve were one flesh, so whatever happened to one would eventually affect the other. When Eve was speaking to the snake, Adam may not have been privy to the conversation directly. Some scholars believe that he was there, while others do not. Some pundits say Adam was so close beside Eve that she gave him some of the fruit she had just eaten (see Genesis 3:6). Yet 1 Timothy 2:14 tells us that Adam was not deceived; Eve was. This may indicate that he was not in the vicinity when she committed this act of disobedience. According to Bible scholar Henry Morris,

> Whether this statement by the Apostle Paul means that Adam was fully aware that he was willfully defying God, or whether it simply means that Adam was not the initial one whom Satan attacked with this deception, may not be completely clear.[3]

Regardless, Adam didn't do anything to stop the disobedience, either because he wasn't there, or he was there and chose not to. Looking at the former, perhaps the couple had a discussion after Eve's encounter with the serpent. The Bible isn't clear concerning how much time passed between her conversation with the devil and the act itself. It could have been years in between. Take into account that Adam and Eve had no knowledge of good and evil at the time, so they probably perceived the snake as friendly. A knowledge of evil would have brought on fear and possibly flight, because they would have viewed the snake as potentially dangerous. Yet Eve never displayed that emotion during her encounter with the snake, according to Scripture. The fear came after the forbidden knowledge was ascertained.

Starve Distractions, Build in Silence

If Satan can get you to feed your distractions, as first Eve and then Adam did, you will begin to starve your focus. Distractions are nourished by your attentiveness to them. So is focus. Your focus is nourished by your attentiveness to it.

On the other hand, your focus is also malnourished by your lack of ability to maintain it. So are distractions. They can be malnourished, too, if you refuse to attend to them. It works both ways.

These things said, you must therefore *starve your distractions and feed your focus.*

You cannot always verbalize the phenomenal things the Lord has in store for you. Nor should you. I sense that the Father is moving on someone reading this at this very moment to construct something without a word. In other words, this is your time to *build in silence.* Don't tell others your plans. This will help you avoid certain distractions. Just let people see the results of your inspired construction. It will speak for you.

Again, you must learn to starve your distractions. You do this by not constantly talking about them. The more you speak of your distractions, the more powerful they will become, eventually resulting in a total loss of focus.

Trust me, I've learned this the hard way. I've made the mistake of not building in silence numerous times. By not feeding my focus and not starving distractions, I opened the door to the enemy, who used other people to take things God had given me (intellectual property, etc.).

People may take your words, but they can't rob you of your anointing. Still, through the multiplicity of your words, people can steal blessings that have your name on them. Proverbs 10:19 (NLT) says, "Too much talk leads to sin. Be sensible and keep your mouth shut." Premature disclosure of information can usurp the Lord's plan for you. To avoid distractions, keep your business to yourself.

Jesus knew this. In one article online, pastor and teacher Nick Cady listed three main instances in the Bible where Jesus instructed people not to tell others who He was or what He had done:

1. After confirming to his disciples that he was indeed the Messiah, Jesus instructed them not to tell anyone. (Matthew 16:20; Mark 8:29–30; Luke 9:20–21)

2. Jesus healed a leper and told him not to tell anyone that he had done this. The man, however, did not comply with this request. (Mark 1:40–44; Matthew 8:1–4; Luke 5:12–15)

3. Jesus told demons not to speak about him and tell others who he was. (Mark 1:34; 3:11–12)[4]

When you speak prematurely about what the Lord has told you, you can sabotage heaven-sent opportunities. The *Merriam-Webster Dictionary* defines *sabotage* as "an act or process tending to hamper or hurt."[5] You must *arrest* the demonic saboteurs in your life. A saboteur is a person (or in this case, a demon) who deliberately damages or destroys things. There are saboteur spirits who reside in or influence individuals to kill your name (reputation) behind closed doors, while those same people smile in your face. I'm very familiar with them.

I recently told a number of people whom I trusted as godly about a choice I had between two tremendous blessings regarding an occupational endeavor. The day I revealed it to a certain so-called friend, all communication about it ceased between us. I didn't hear back about the opportunity for several days. When I did, it was via an email telling me that the business would not be proceeding with me in the venture. I blame my big mouth! I had forgotten that this person was notorious for upending others' blessings with malicious words spoken against those whom he or she didn't like. The individual had a reputation of acting like a friend, but was irrefutably an enemy in disguise.

When people do you wrong, and some will, don't let it bother you or stop godly progress. This is your season to reset your emotions and not allow them to control your movement. You can effectively do this by not revealing your blessings before their time. When you change your circle of people, trust and believe that you will also change your life.

Don't allow the enemy to steal your focus. Some people have allowed their distraction to become their god by focusing more on the problem than on the solution the Lord provides. They don't inquire of Him for the answer because the distraction has dominated their thought processes. As I mentioned before, the enemy's primary target of attack is your mind. If he can take your attention off God and redirect it to whatever is currently distracting you, he wins that battle. No matter what you're going through today, don't let the devil hinder you with demonic distractions. Stay focused on God, not your current situation. In fact, your current condition is not your final end if you keep your mind stayed on the Lord. Glory!

Undisturbed and Unbothered

The enemy is doing his best to bother you. He is causing circumstances—all kinds of disturbances such as health issues, car accidents, family illnesses, financial hardship, etc.—to keep you from heading in the direction of your destiny. These distractions have been assaulting your potential testimonies in an effort to prevent you from making the correct decisions. Like Jesus, you must keep writing in the sand as the accuser of the brethren speaks curses against you and others in the background:

> This they said, testing Him, that they might have something of which to accuse Him. But Jesus stooped down and wrote on the ground with His finger, as though He did not hear.
> So when they continued asking Him, He raised Himself up and said to them, "He who is without sin among you, let him throw a stone at her first." And again He stooped down and wrote on the ground.
>
> John 8:6–8

Don't even look in the enemy's direction; keep writing in the sand, undisturbed and unbothered. If you happen to glance at him, rebuke him (see Zechariah 3:2). Jesus did, and so can you!

In Matthew 8:23–27, Jesus and the disciples were out on the water when a storm rocked their boat. It was a satanic interruption that had to be rebuked. Rebuke your distractions in Jesus' name, and focus on Him. While you're going through trials and tribulations, keep your eyes on the Lord. I decree laser-like focus for you, although hell may be breaking out all around you at this time. When the devil is roaring at you, ignore him. I declare, in the strength of the Lord, that you will finish the ministerial assignment, the book, or whatever you're called of God to do. Tell the devil that you will not be moved by what your eyes see or what your heart experiences. You will stay focused on that which the Lord has called you to, knowing that the bigger the distraction, the greater the call of the Lord.

I heard this in my spirit for you: *Don't let it bother you!* Be unbothered by your current condition. It's not your conclusion. Don't let distractions rent a room in your mind. If they've already secured a room, then evict them in Jesus' name. Serve an eviction notice to the enemy. The test you're currently going through will transform into a testimony. Wait, watch, and see!

The Distraction of Social Media

Nowadays, the enemy is using social media and other technology as a distraction. For example, suppose you've decided to write the book that the Lord placed in your spirit years ago. Almost every time you attempt to sit down and write it, you decide to look at your social media page for a moment. The next thing you know, you're posting, commenting, and responding to argumentative people.

Before you know it, you've been going back and forth for almost an hour with one person who negatively commented on your post. After getting off social media, you realize that you didn't begin the manuscript that you were so determined to write. Why? You allowed yourself to get distracted.

This happens often. Again, it's no accident. Demons know how to influence your flesh. They are able to identify what you like because they watch you.

If you don't separate yourself from your distractions, these evil spirits will begin to separate you from your godly mandate. Demons of distraction can be so loud in their interference that they can prevent you from hearing the Lord's voice when you need to hear Him the most.

Walk over Adversity

Don't get distracted by circumstances. In Matthew 14:26–31, the twelve disciples were on a boat and saw Jesus walking on the sea. They assumed that He was a spirit (a ghost), and fear gripped them. The Lord reassured them that He was not.

Peter, the boldest of the group, wanted to walk to Jesus on the water. The Messiah told him, "Come." Peter stepped out of the boat and started walking on water to get to Jesus, but the wind and waves distracted him so that he shifted his focus from his Lord. He then began to sink. Thankfully, Jesus saved him, but consequently He questioned Peter's faith.

You must operate like a horse with blinders on, not looking to the left or right, but straight ahead. You must *walk over adversity* like Peter, except that you will not take your eyes or focus off Christ Jesus. With distraction comes doubt, which is a result of the enemy getting you to look at your current situation instead of your Lord. The aftereffect of this may be sinking in discouragement, because you may feel as if your faith wasn't up to par. Discouragement and distraction have a symbiotic relationship in the spirit. Distraction can lead to discouragement by creating feelings of failure in people when they don't complete a godly assignment.

Whatever your assignment from God, *keep walking, keep plowing.* The enemy will sometimes use people and their hate to try to stop what God has started. The devil will use other people's negative talk, their exclusion of you, and their dislike to distract you. You must use their hatred to increase your love for them, for God, and for His people. *Let your haters be your elevators* in this season of your life.

Don't involve yourself in the foolishness of others. Focus on what God has called you to do. If you do that, you will walk into a season of accomplishments. Don't allow demonic distractions to dissuade you. Finish what you've started. Allow the enemy's hatred to push you into greater heights in the Lord.

Remember, the devil's attacks are really backhanded compliments. He'd leave you and your family alone if you weren't a threat. *I've never seen a thief hang around an empty vault.* Satan knows that something of value is in you. He has a sneaking suspicion that you will build God's Kingdom and tear down his own.

The Distraction of the Opposite Sex

Demons will most assuredly use the opposite sex to distract you. They're not going to present you with something unappealing, but rather with what you like. This can happen when you surf the worldwide web or a social media site and accidentally see something or someone inappropriate that draws your attention. You stop to watch the video, and it immediately undermines your focus.

Each time this happens, Satan is actually planting seeds. The video that you saw doesn't necessarily have to be pornographic, just someone that's eye-catching. Next, much of the time you once spent focused on the Lord is now spent being entertained by the opposite sex. Don't think that you are the only one who has struggled with this. This type of distraction has affected a few people in Scripture. The mighty Samson was distracted by the beauty of Delilah (see Judges 16). This eventually led him to reveal the secret of his uncanny strength to her, which in the long run cost him his life.

The chosen king and prophet of God, David, son of Jesse, was also distracted by a woman bathing herself: "Then it happened one evening that David arose from his bed and walked on the roof of the king's house. And from the roof he saw a woman bathing, and the woman was very beautiful to behold" (2 Samuel 11:2). Struck by her beauty, David felt that he had to have her. The woman's name was Bathsheba, and she just happened to be Uriah the Hittite's wife. David took her from her husband, resulting in the conception of a child.

Ungodly soul ties created by immoral activities between two adults have led to the downfall of many. The devil orchestrates such unions to eventually destroy the individuals. This even happened to God's chosen king. David tried to hide his sin and even arranged the killing of Uriah, an honest and faithful man, in battle (see 2 Samuel 11:15). After the murder of Bathsheba's husband, David's hidden sins, which had first begun as a distraction by the opposite sex, were exposed by the prophet Nathan:

> Why have you despised the commandment of the LORD, to do evil in His sight? You have killed Uriah the Hittite with the sword; you have taken his wife to be your wife, and have killed him with the sword of the people of Ammon. Now therefore, the sword shall never depart from your house, because you have despised Me, and have taken the wife of Uriah the Hittite to be your wife.
>
> 2 Samuel 12:9–10

In David's case, a huge distraction gave way to egregious sins, resulting in the sword never departing from his house. Though he repented numerous times, the king still had to face the consequences of his actions. The *Benson Commentary* explains 2 Samuel 12:10 further:

The sword shall never depart from thy house—During the residue of thy life. As long as he [David] lived, at times there should be destruction made in his family by the sword, which was awfully fulfilled in the violent deaths of his children, Amnon and Absalom, and, about the time of his death, Adonijah.[6]

According to this same verse, when David took Bathsheba from Uriah, it showed a hatred for the laws or rules of God: "you have despised Me." That's why calamity plagued the king and his household for the rest of their lives.

Satan was involved and set David up to be distracted by the opposite sex all those years ago. His tactics haven't changed. He is doing the same things today. Don't let distractions by the opposite sex lead you into sin. If you do, you may have to pay an enormous price.

Ministry Can Be a Mistress

Believe it or not, the ministry can even bring distractions. If a husband spends more time ministering in the Church than ministering to his wife, then he may possibly have a mistress. If a married woman spends more time attending to her pastor's needs than to her husband's, then she might have a paramour. In both cases, the unfaithful partner has allowed ministry to become a major distraction. I have seen this destroy a lot of marriages.

Contrary to popular opinion, family is your first ministry. Paul's advice to his spiritual son Timothy in the Bible emphasizes this: "But if anyone does not provide for his own family, especially for his own household, he has denied the faith and is worse than an unbeliever" (1 Timothy 5:8 csb).

The devil can and often does use the *busyness* of church as a distraction. Some wives will cook for the entire congregation, but refuse to do the same for their spouse and children. Some men will travel the world as itinerant ministers, but spend very little time with their families. I was guilty of this. One year, I traveled so much for ministry that my youngest daughter, Jayla, said, "Daddy, you're never home on the weekend."

Jayla's words hit me to my core. I canceled all the ministry engagements I could for the rest of that year so I could spend more quality time with my spouse and daughters. If I fail to minister to my biological family, I have failed as a minister of the Gospel. My itinerary is hectic now, but I consistently push to spend more time with my loved ones.

In the Bible, Martha was distracted by ministry. As you read the following passage, take into account that to *minister* means to wait on others, support and care for them, and attend to them.

As Jesus and the disciples continued on their way to Jerusalem, they came to a certain village where a woman named Martha welcomed him into her home. Her sister, Mary, sat at the Lord's feet, listening to what he taught. But Martha was distracted by the big dinner she was preparing. She came to Jesus and said, "Lord, doesn't it seem unfair to you that my sister just sits here while I do all the work? Tell her to come and help me."

But the Lord said to her, "My dear Martha, you are worried and upset over all these details! There is only one thing worth being concerned about. Mary has discovered it, and it will not be taken away from her."

Luke 10:38–42 NLT

Martha was distracted with dinner preparations, while Mary stayed in the presence of Jesus, receiving His instructions. Although both their services were necessary, Mary sought the Lord first. She wouldn't allow herself to focus on anything except Him.

Unfortunately, with some people ministry is not always about Jesus, but about themselves. As I mentioned in chapter 5, sometimes pride is involved. As with Lucifer, pride comes before destruction and an arrogant spirit before a fall (see Proverbs 16:18).

If you are in ministry, don't ever allow it to take your focus off Jesus. When you refuse to be distracted, God will bring you *divine attractions* (a draw to things that He approves of). Don't allow the *spirit of distraction* to divert you from your destiny. It's an energy waster, a time stealer, a peace drainer, and a ministry derailer. We can accomplish so much in ministry if we don't allow this spirit to have illegal authority over us. Its main goal is to keep you in an arena called *unfinished business*. Its desire is to keep you occupied so that you never finish your business for God. Don't let satanically planned diversions hinder your progress. This is your time to let go of every malignant or cancerous spirit that keeps you focused on flesh over spirit.

Purposeful Distractions

I just heard the word *WAR* in my spirit. You may have been viewing a single battle as an all-out war. It is not. There is a difference between the two. A battle is one encounter between opposing forces. A war is a conflict on a larger scale, between nations, or between two or more states within a country.

You must first address the battles in your own neighborhood before you war for your nation. There is an order to spiritual combat and a hierarchy in Satan's kingdom. Demonic forces will retaliate if you come ill-equipped for either a battle or the war. You can win a single battle (or even more than one), yet still lose the war.

Child of God, pick and choose your battles. Some conflicts are purposeful distractions that keep you from completing the Lord's purpose in your life. The enemy uses these unnecessary and meaningless skirmishes to keep you engrossed with winning a battle, so that you lose the war. But be encouraged! Keep on fighting, with the larger purpose of the Father for you always in view. With each battle you successfully get through, the weight of your future blessings increases.

Rejoice in Your Rainy Season

This word I am hearing in my spirit is for someone reading this. If it's you, receive the following:

Do what the Lord has instructed you to do. When you do, you'll experience the turnaround and blessings you've been waiting for. I see that you've been running from your assignment, like the prophet Jonah. God is shaking up your boat and allowing you to be thrown off for a purpose (see Jonah 1:11–13). While in the water, initially you tried to stay afloat by your own power and will. You were then swallowed up by the very problems that hid your promise. Know that these issues were purposely sent by the Lord to transport you to where He was trying to get you to go. On your continued journey to this place, you will hear His voice as never before during your time in the *belly of adversity*. Free from distractions, you'll be situated in the *belly of the beast* long enough to truly listen to what He has been saying to you all along. This beast will be used to take you to your assigned place (see Jonah 2:10). God is allowing your problems to move you closer to what He wants you to do. When you are released, you will have gained a new perspective and resolve to declare what "thus saith the Lord" (see Jonah 2:10). Then and only then will the deluge of blessings God has been holding back because of disobedience fall on you like rain. Before, the sea (issues) completely encompassed you. But when you reach dry land—and the Lord will bring you there—the rain (blessings) will be falling upon you. I see you being naturally and spiritually renewed. Rejoice in your season of rain!

YOUR BATTLE PLAN

You must maintain laser-like focus, although hell is breaking out all around you—these are only distractions. They are temporary inconveniences that will not last forever. The enemy's desire is to provide intense distractions in order to steal your focus. Don't let him. Refuse to be distracted, and the Lord will provide heavenly attractions for you. Cut off any and every demonic soul tie, especially from your past. Activate the strength of the Lord through prayer, fasting, worship, and reading His Word daily so you can restart, reset, and finish the assignment of the Lord, whether it be writing a book, carrying out a ministerial call, accomplishing a business venture—whatever you've been divinely called to do. When you are praying, fasting, worshiping, and reading God's Word, you won't be so easily distracted by demons and will learn how to keep your eyes focused on Christ Jesus.

YOUR BATTLE PRAYER

Father God, I am determined not to lose my focus on what you've called me to do. I bind every hex, vex, voodoo, hoodoo, juju, and curse from hell that attacks my focus and strengthens my distractions. Lord, may those people who have distracted me also exit my life, without me saying a word to them. As I change my circle, it will reduce demonic distractions. I will be unbothered by the multiplicity of diversions that the legions of hell may send, or by the people whom hell might use. I will keep my focus on Jesus and what He has charged me to do.

Father, don't let Satan distract me for his purposes. Allow me to maintain my focus on your blessed Son, Jesus. If I ever feel my concentration on you wavering, give me the fortitude and resilience to fast so that you will show me how to regain it. I will keep plowing in the natural and in the spirit. I make a covenant with my eyes so that I won't be distracted by the opposite sex. I cast out any spirit of pride within me that I discover through prayerful introspection. During my times of prayer, I will not be distracted by social media.

I will focus on making time spent with you sacred and distraction-free. I pray all of this in the mighty name of my Lord and Savior, Jesus Christ. Hallelujah!

(Note: Begin praising God in order to seal this prayer in the heavens.)

Technology: The Devil Is in the Details

And he had power to give life unto the image of the beast, that the image of the beast should both speak, and cause that as many as would not worship the image of the beast should be killed.

—Revelation 13:15 KJV

While high-tech advancements have been a great boon to humankind, the devil is definitely in the details. Demonic spirits have the innate ability to make use of inanimate objects, and computerized devices are no exception. In the Scripture you just read, I believe that "the image of the beast" refers to a highly sophisticated supercomputer, very much like the ones we can hold in the palm of our hand today. These powerful devices that once took up entire buildings have become so small that they can actually fit in our pockets. Computer-based devices have become such an intricate and intimate part of most of our lives that we can hardly imagine life without them.

Scripture lets us know that the contrivances of technology are neither evil nor good; their use for either is based on who or what uses them. Jason Thacker, an expert in the field of ethics in technology, wrote,

> Nowhere in Scripture is a tool or a technology condemned for being evil. Scripture shows that technology and tools can be used for both good and evil. Even if a tool was designed for evil, the tool itself isn't evil. What is sinful isn't the sword but how people choose to use it. It can be used for righteous purposes like standing up for justice against those who are evil, but it can also be used to hurt or kill the innocent. While technology isn't moral in that sense, it does carry with it the effects of sin and brokenness. Technology is not morally neutral, because it influences and changes us each time we use it.[1]

Technology "influences and changes us each time we use it." What a powerful statement by Jason Thacker. It actually does! The more we use technology, the more dependent we become on it. For instance, could you imagine going without your smartphone for a month? Oh, the horror! Satan knows this and exploits it to his advantage.

In Ephesians 2:2, the devil is called the "prince of the power of the air." This means that the enemy of our soul has power and authority over the atmosphere. In Ephesians 6:11–12, the apostle Paul also admonishes us to put on the whole armor of God and contend against the spiritual hosts of wickedness in what we could call the "regions of the air": "For we are not fighting against flesh-and-blood enemies, but against evil rulers and authorities of the unseen world, against mighty powers in this dark world, and against evil spirits in the heavenly places" (Ephesians 6:12 NLT).

This foul ruling spirit, Satan, oversees the demonic principalities that make their abode in hell and in the troposphere that surrounds the earth. The troposphere "provides oxygen that we can breathe, keeps Earth at a livable temperature, and allows for weather to occur, making it a very important part of the atmosphere."[2] When we study various electronic developments, we find that many of them, particularly the worldwide web, are reliant on the air. In the same manner that air is our constant companion, thousands of devils besiege us from that region on a daily basis. They are not omnipresent, but they are, like the air, always present within an environment that is conducive to them.

For example, an authentic, anointed church worship service would prove suffocating for a demon because the air becomes saturated with the supernatural glory of the Most High. That's why you will see so many spontaneous demonic manifestations, reactions, and expulsions in this kind of setting. I have witnessed this myself on various occasions. When God's presence invades a Spirit-led gathering, devils flee in absolute terror. Praise the Lord! God and His angels are in the air too.

According to experts at the University of Delaware, information is transmitted through the internet via two basic methods: wires and frequency waves through the air. One of their articles explains transmission through the air this way: "Microwaves are high-frequency waves that travel through the air in order to transmit data. . . . Microwaves can travel directly through the air to each individual host, or are relayed all around the world through satellites."[3] If the internet is primarily transmitted through frequency waves over the air, then we shouldn't be surprised that Satan holds great influence over what's delivered via the "information highway." For example, have you ever innocently surfed the web and had pornographic material pop up? Trust me when I tell you that this is not accidental. It is Satan's carefully planned strategy to allow demonic intrusion primarily through your eye and ear gates.

Guard Your Gates and Hedges

It is very important to guard every gate in your life (your eyes, ears, mouth, etc.) meticulously to keep evil spirits from permeating it.

The devil continuously looks for entry points to defile you. Gates and hedges have very similar functions. They are both designed to protect in the natural and spiritual domains.

In the first chapter of the book of Job, the devil had obviously attempted to breach the hedge of protection that the Lord had placed around Job, his family, and his property. We know about this protection because of what we read in verse 10, where Satan asks the Lord, "Have You not made a hedge around him, around his household, and around all that he has on every side?"

Hedge in Hebrew means "wall,"[4] which indicates a certain level of protection for the believer. Jeff Cranston, pastor of Low Country Community Church, wrote in his blog "Hedge of Protection,"

> As seen with Job, a hedge is an apt illustration for what God's protection looks like. . . .
>
> We can allow Satan and his demons to breach the hedge by our carelessness of leaving the gate open, through a direct or indirect invitation to demonic powers, through sins of commission and omission, through holes left unrepaired after sins are confessed and forgiven, etc. Even if there are no other reasons, God may allow demons to breach the hedge, as He did with Job, for purposes of testing, learning, or other Divine Reasons that only God may know.[5]

Cranston provides great wisdom about the way that *snakes* (demons) breach our hedges through unclosed gates. Never allow the gates of your hedges to remain open, be left unguarded, or be penetrated.

Shake the Hedge, Evict the Snake

Pastor Janis Heiser of River of Life Fellowship Church in Lock Haven, Pennsylvania, wrote that in biblical times,

Hedges were made of low, intertwined thorn bushes that would grow around what needed to be protected and used similar to a fence to keep out wild animals, especially from livestock.
     However, there could still be some danger. It was very common for someone to pick up a stick and hit the corner of the hedge, to see a snake come slithering out![6]

The King James Version of the Bible says in Ecclesiastes 10:8 that "whoso breaketh an hedge, a serpent shall bite him." The New International Version words it as "whoever breaks through a wall may be bitten by a snake." Whenever a hedge (wall) of protection is broken through, a snake may bite you! The serpent is commonly identified as the evil one, Satan, in the Bible. Our hedges must be shaken in order to dislodge any snakes that have made their home within the branches of the thorn bushes, waiting for an opening to strike. The snakes (demons) in the hedge are dislodged through spiritual warfare. This happens when they are confronted by a deliverance minister or a true believer. Before they are expelled, the shaking causes them to manifest. This shaking will eliminate the element of surprise on the part of the devil. Instead of the snake being able to attack when the hedge is broken, the shaking of the hedge beforehand exposes the chief demon so that you can break him.
     In the spiritual realm, keep in mind that a hedge is a protective fence or barrier the Lord builds around a person and his/her family (household) and possessions. As Cranston pointed out, "Job couldn't see the hedge, but Satan could!"[7] It's a comforting reminder to know that while a hedge can be unseen by us, it's quite clearly seen by the emissaries of evil. In Job 1:8–10 (AMP), the Bible provides evidence that hell is cognizant of the believer's hedges:

The LORD said to Satan, "Have you considered and reflected on My servant Job? For there is none like him on the earth, a blameless and upright man, one who fears God [with reverence] and abstains from and turns away from evil [because he honors God]." Then Satan answered the LORD, "Does Job fear God for nothing? Have You not put a hedge [of protection] around him and his house and all that he has, on every side? You have blessed the work of his hands [and conferred prosperity and happiness upon him], and his possessions have increased in the land."

The Lord allowed Lucifer to test this man of God; He gave Lucifer permission to penetrate Job's hedge and take all he had amassed in his lifetime, even his health. As I mentioned in chapter 4, in 1998, after I had backslidden for a number of years, the Lord spoke to my spirit, saying that if I didn't choose to follow Him fully, He would remove the protective spiritual hedge I'd had my entire life and leave me to my own devices, mindset, and will. I sensed that if I didn't obey His instructions, then I'd be on my own. When Job's hedge was infiltrated, his wife and friends pretty much left him on his own. He temporarily lost the confidence of his unnamed wife and friends. (I refer to Job's wife as unnamed because in all my years of ministry, I've never heard anyone refer to her by name. I found out in my research that a name for her is never mentioned in Scripture; she is always simply "Job's wife.")

Job was blessed because there was no one like him in his era, according to the Lord. Job was the real deal. He was righteous and principled. Job reverenced the Lord and eschewed evil in exchange for venerating God. That was the secret to his prosperity. It can be our secret as well. But if we're not careful, we may, like Job, lose everything: our offspring, assets, and health.

Satan Infiltrated Job's Technology

To relate how the enemy used tools of technology when assailing Job, I want to focus on the loss of his sheep, camels, oxen, and female donkeys. Let's also look at the number of these animals

Job had. Because numbers have such profound meaning in the Bible, I believe his future was prophesied in Job chapter 1 mainly based on the number of animals he possessed at the start. This is interesting because the maintenance of his livestock was tied to his use of the "technology" of his day, which included a rod, staff, plow, axe, hammer, anvil, and file, just to name a few of the things he used.

Job 1:3 gives us the numbers: "Also, his possessions were seven thousand sheep, three thousand camels, five hundred yoke of oxen, five hundred female donkeys, and a very large household, so that this man was the greatest of all the people of the East." In this sacred Scripture, Job's favorable outcome was prophesied before his attack from Satan even began. In actuality, it indicated that he would receive double grace at the end of all the devastation he and his family would suffer.

Let me explain. In my study of the Bible, the number 7 often refers to the completion or end of a cycle. The number 3 connotes being complete, whole, or in a state of perfection. The number 5 indicates God's grace, or a level of favor that supersedes our ability to earn it.[8] In this same verse of Job, we see all of these numbers, and the number 5 is mentioned twice, which indicates a double portion of favor, blessings, and restoration. Job successfully completed his examination from the Lord, and in the end he received double of everything, including the livestock mentioned in Job 1:3 that he had lost due to unprovoked Satanic interference.

Again, the tools Job used to manage the livestock and land were the technology of his day. The animals represented his family's godly economy and were a significant part of the prosperity and "great household" status the family enjoyed. By eliminating these animals, the enemy could destroy Job's prodigious wealth. Satan believed that when he removed the blessing of Job's finances, this righteous man would blaspheme Jehovah. Satan told God this was what Job would do.

With the destruction of the animals, people, and Job's health, his great household fell. Satan couldn't attack Job directly, because the Lord had restricted his demonic harassment (see Job 1:12). But he was successful in eliminating Job's livelihood, rendering his acquired technology useless. In a sense, this was an infection of that day's technology because Job had nothing left to use it on. Yet this strategy, in which the devil attempted to get Job to curse God to His face, failed miserably.

Getting you to curse your Creator for your calamity is one of Satan's tactics for getting you to look to him as your source instead of the Lord. But God is our source. Everything else is a resource. Through all Job went through, he cursed everything in his life but God. So Satan was wrong about him.

"Stay alert! Watch out for your great enemy, the devil. He prowls around like a roaring lion, looking for someone to devour" (1 Peter 5:8 NLT). If you can withstand Satan's attack, I believe that like Job, double can also be your portion. You need to grab this word for yourself. If you are going through tremendous testing at this very moment, limit any complaining. Job complained throughout the majority of the Bible book about him, and I believe this kept him in his sorry state longer. The moment that he stopped complaining, however, was the moment that he received double what he had before. Complaining can keep you from your promise, just as it did the children of Israel. It kept them out of the Promised Land for years. Rest assured that if you limit your complaining during trying times, the end result will be twice what you had before. God is able and ready to supply you with heavenly technology that will replace the demonic or counterfeit tech of the enemy.

Get Off That Phone!

If the devil can infiltrate yesterday's technology, he can do the same with today's, especially smartphones. I've written this section to help you receive deliverance from your smartphone. I'm joking, sort of, but not really. Have you ever seen someone manifest demonically when his or her smartphone was lost, stolen, or taken away? Ever experience a time when you went to work, only to realize that you left your smartphone at home? Did you go back home to get it? I did, more than once. We seem to have an unnatural, synergetic relationship with these devices. Amen? (I knew I wouldn't get too many amens on that one!)

As a Chicago Public Schools teacher for over thirty years, I have witnessed quite a few students become exceptionally unruly when threatened with having their phones taken away. They would become argumentative, defiant, and in some cases, violent. This is an unnatural "disease" that has affected much of the world's population. I believe we've all been affected.

To be totally transparent, one of the first things I do upon waking in the morning is to reach sleepily for my smartphone. I instinctively check my missed calls, texts, voicemails, emails, social media posts, and comments. Most people probably do the same. As a believer, I should be reaching for my Bible, but instead, it's my phone. This clearly shows how dominant technology has become in our lives.

I'm the first to admit to my admiration for the modern-day conveniences that we enjoy today. Yet here, I must address the dangers, as well as technology's connection to the end times. Whether we know it or not, we are living in the last days. Our Lord will soon return. This is quite evident just by watching what's going on in the world. All the chaos, murder, and crime that we see bear witness to this fact. Author Tony Reinke states,

> For those with eyes to see, Christ's return is so imminent, it potently declutters our lives of everything that is superficial and renders all our vain distractions irrelevant. To put it another way, our battle against the encumbering distractions of this world—especially the unnecessary distractions of our phones—is a heart

war we can wage only if our affections are locked firmly on the glory of Christ.[9]

Our phones are a blessing, but they're also a distraction. Some people have unknowingly anointed their phones as gods over their lives. Others have an almost reverent, yet abnormal relationship with their mobile devices. It's not a stretch at all to link such behavior with the demonic realm. Anything a person does that is uncharacteristically habitual, meaning that you can't do without it for too long—food, alcohol, smoking, sex, etc.—usually has a demon of addiction behind it. This includes our mobile devices. Addictions are usually hidden. This can be true of our phones as well. As Tony Reinke said, it's a *heart war*. Our affections should be centered on the Lord above technological advances.

A Secret War

The devil has initiated a *secret war* that he is waging in most of our children's bedrooms. When our kids are locked away in their rooms with their beloved smartphones in hand, it presents an opportunity for demonic intrusion. With the advent of social media, today's youth have more access to pornography, illicit adult content, Satanic indoctrination, violence, and profanity than previous generations ever did. My three daughters have this same access, and trust me when I say that it has been a battle for my wife and me. Parents who are reading this must be extremely vigilant about the content their kids are viewing. As parents, we cannot allow the serpent to have access to our babies. We must prevent temptation before it becomes sin that could possibly lead to death, according to Romans 6:23.

Some biblical scholars believe that Satan was cast out of heaven after the creation of the angels and before the time of Adam and Eve (see Isaiah 14:12–14; Ezekiel 28:12–18). In Genesis 3, as we saw previously, the snake convinced Eve to eat of the Tree of Knowledge of Good and Evil, which God had expressly told Adam they must not do. Satan is still trying to get our children to disobey God, but he has just changed locations. Instead of the Garden of Eden, he infiltrates our homes, schools, workplaces, and technology. When our kids are alone with their smartphones, that's when the serpent speaks the loudest.

You and I can't afford to make the same mistake that the first two humans on the planet made. When they obeyed the snake and disobeyed God, their eyes were opened. They were impregnated with the knowledge of good and evil. Fathers and mothers, we are the watchmen of our offspring. We have to pay heed to what they are seeing. Satan's army is limited, with a fixed total number of soldiers. They don't have the ability to reproduce, only to copy or imitate. Demons are not omnipresent, but they strive to be, through current technology. Let's be vigilant in terms of monitoring serpent spirits that are slithering around looking for an opportunity to infect our children's use of their devices. "Lest Satan should take advantage of us; for we are not ignorant of his devices" (2 Corinthians 2:11).

Have you ever heard the phrase *a ghost in the machine*? It's spiritually true when it comes to smartphones. For the record, ghosts are demons (read my book *Supernaturally Delivered* for more information on this subject). In my opinion, demons don't just inhabit humans and animals; they can also attach their influence to inanimate objects like technological devices.

Please understand, I'm not saying that all technological breakthroughs are evil. I'm saying that Satan is using many of them to seduce a new generation. In fact, he manipulates demonically charged people to use his devices for the detriment of society. Numerous children have been led astray by pedophiles, deviants, rapists, perverts, and the like invading their bedrooms through smartphones. Young girls have been seduced by older men via their phones. This is one of the tactics the devil uses in an attempt to destroy the lives of our kids. As the leaders of our homes, we have to rise up against this assault and let Satan know that he cannot have our families, in Jesus' name!

The devil has the ability to speak to you and your loved ones through computer devices and apps. If he can do so through people, why not through technology that has the ability to communicate with you and the rest of the world? In Revelation 13:15, the antichrist gave power to the image of the beast to both live and speak. Thus, this beast—which I see as technology, particularly artificial intelligence (or AI)—is speaking to a copious number of people now through machines we use regularly that are right under our noses. The beast's goal is to get you to worship it.

Unfortunately, some people actually worship the beast without truly realizing it, as I mentioned earlier. As a result, a great spiritual falling away is occurring within the world today. We must never worship the creation more than the Creator, but that is occurring in our day. As I mentioned in chapter 4, the ultimate goal of the god of this age is to kill us spiritually. We cannot allow him to do so. The way to stop this is to identify his methodologies and be armed with a battle plan to stop them. That's one of the reasons I wrote this book.

What Is Artificial Intelligence?

IBM provides the following definition of artificial intelligence (AI): "Artificial intelligence leverages computers and machines to mimic the problem-solving and decision-making capabilities of the human mind."[10] Again, I equate the beast mentioned in Revelation 13:15 to technology, or more succinctly, to artificial intelligence.

Artificial intelligence is all the rage right now. Just ask Siri, or say "Hey, Google" to your computer device or smart television, and both can thoroughly explain its value. Both utilize use this technology. AI is becoming so popular that some people use it regularly without even realizing it. It's in homes, workplaces, churches, etc. AI software can be downloaded through computer applications and embedded in smart devices, including the GPS (Global Positioning System) in automobiles, as well as a host of other technologies. AI has the ability to speak to us, write for us, and think for us, along with numerous other functions.

As electronic machinery progresses, a very real possibility exists that in time, it will become sentient or self-aware. If this occurs, AI devices will be ripe for internal habitation by the fallen angels, demons, or Nephilim. I'll explain more about the Nephilim shortly. Briefly here, let me add that the fallen angels spoken of in Revelation 12:7–10 are those who followed Lucifer in rebellion against God and were cast out of heaven. Some theologians believe that these fallen angels are demons, but according to 2 Peter 2:4, they are bound in hell until Judgment Day. The Nephilim mentioned in Genesis 6:4, however, were the "giants" that walked the earth long ago and had sexual relations with the daughters of humans. In my research, I've found that some scholars are of the opinion that demons are the disembodied spirits of the Nephilim.

We are currently inundated with a myriad of AI apps that have the ability to learn from us and steal our jobs, in addition to their previously mentioned functions. High school and college students around the country use AI technology to complete their reports, term papers, quizzes, and tests. The enemy can easily use this tool to manipulate us and lead us further from the Word of God (Jesus).

If, as I have always believed, the beast mentioned in Revelation 13:15 is analogous to some type of supercomputer or more advanced form of technology, then the relatively new emergence of artificial intelligence fits the bill. AI now has the power to write books, hold human-like conversations, create art, and engage in a host of other activities. But when we hold conversations with apps or devices that use AI, whom are we really speaking to? Remember, artificial intelligence mimics or counterfeits the human brain. Its creators are giving this tech the power to "live" and to speak.

Elon Musk, chief executive of Tesla Inc. and SpaceX, and co-founder of Neuralink and OpenAI, said the following: "With artificial intelligence, we are summoning the demon."[11] Musk, one of the wealthiest men on the planet, stated that AI is "potentially more dangerous than nukes."[12] It has the potential to take a self-appointed role as a global peacekeeper or become our "Uber nanny." I agree with Musk in this particular case. As time progresses, AI will become more and more dominant in the management of world affairs. Nuclear war, financial institution shutdowns, food shortages, recessions, depressions, and the like could be orchestrated by demons that reside in the hardware and software of its ersatz DNA.

We have recently seen this with the system-wide shutdown of AT&T, causing millions of people to be without cellular service for a total of six hours, including me. The U.S. House of Representatives just recently passed a bill, H.R. 7521, that is designed to "protect the national security of the United States from the threat posed by foreign adversary controlled applications, such as TikTok" (due to China's suspected infiltration of that popular app).[13] As of this writing, the U.S. Senate has yet to pass this bill. Today, I went to get breakfast at my local McDonald's and couldn't order because their computer systems were down. This kind of technological interference may sound like science fiction, but it is speedily becoming science fact. I believe that the next world war will take place in the cyber world before it manifests in the natural one. It will begin with some of the aforementioned events above, but I'm reassured by the fact that the Lord will always provide a way of escape for His people.

The Rise of the Robots

In the not-so-distant future, we could see machines that think and act like "human beings" and are physically almost indistinguishable from us. They will be dependent on the burgeoning AI technology of today. However, these robotic creations could easily be inhabited by demons. These automatons will eliminate much of the *Homo sapiens* workforce, as their inferior counterparts are doing currently. This will cause vast unemployment worldwide.

As to future employment, the upcoming generation should concentrate on careers or trades that robots cannot perform. Satan will be behind many of the future technological breakthroughs that reduce the need for humans. His goal is to eliminate the Lord's greatest creation: *you*. What seems like a great technological boon may end up being the vehicle Satan uses for global destruction.

Is it really that far-fetched for demons to speak to you and me through AI? Isn't this what's happening in the modern age when it comes to AI? Demonic entities have definitely become the puppet masters that pull the strings of certain segments of technology behind the scenes.

Root spirits are demonic spirits that aren't readily seen. Like roots in the natural, they're underground—unseen until dug up. They nourish demonic seeds, which is why we need to identify the root spirits of the technology crisis before they germinate. These include:

1. Isolation
2. Loneliness
3. Boredom
4. Escapism

I mentioned in chapter 1 that the best environment in which to hear the voice of God is the wilderness, where you're all alone (see Matthew 4:1–11). But when you're isolated, you will hear not only His voice but also Satan's. Jesus heard them both in the wilderness and in various times of isolation in Scripture. A *spirit of isolation* or *spirit of separation* seeks to get you off by yourself so that it can speak to you unimpeded and uninterrupted. Employing the gift of discerning of spirits is paramount here (see

1 Corinthians 12:10) because it's how you will know whether a time of separation for conversation is orchestrated by the Lord or the enemy. Keep in mind that gifts are given freely by definition, even by the Father. All you have to do is ask for them.

In isolation, the *spirit of loneliness* may start to build up in a person. The enemy plays on this. He exacerbates that emotion, leading an individual to reach out to technology (i.e., a tablet, computer, smartphone, etc.), which provides access to various social media websites or apps. This temporarily relieves the loneliness by connecting the person with others online.

The *spirit of boredom*, a fraternal twin of loneliness, is related to it but can look quite different. It provides the fuel to push a person into demonic realms. Access to social media, for example, starts with a way in. It could be by signing in, along with entering a password. Once you're in, you may encounter demonic influences, or godly ones. The technological world is very similar to the natural world in that respect, but its gates or entry points are composed of waves, sound, light, and frequencies.

This all gives way to a *spirit of escapism*, which is on full display on virtual reality platforms. You are placed in a computer-generated environment instead of being an active participant outside it. This is extremely dangerous because it can create a false perception of reality and can be very addictive. Some users will ultimately start to prefer this alternate pseudo-world over the real one, thus spending more and more time in it. Within this environment, demonic spirits potentially can become life educators, leading many astray from the Gospel of Jesus Christ. In this way, the evil one can get his clutches on a person more completely. We cannot allow this to happen. The key is to recognize his plan so that you can avoid his traps.

As I wrote earlier, however, technology itself is not intrinsically evil or good. Its use either way is solely based on the user. There are many people sharing the glorious Gospel of Jesus Christ in the virtual world and leading souls to Him.

Social Media Games and Quizzes

Have you ever casually perused your main feed on a social media website and had online games, quizzes, and surveys pop up? I have. Did you ever use apps on social media to make you look younger or older? I have. Some of the results have been quite shocking. Other online video games deal with psychic phenomena, gambling, demons, astrology, crime, and more. They have sadly become the new psychics and mediums of this era. I believe that evil intentions are behind many of these games and quizzes. There are people who innocently participate in them, only to find out later that it was to their detriment. Some quizzes are actually used to harvest your personal information, steal your identity, and get you to share your results with friends and family. On one well-known social media website, 63,000 user accounts were compromised in one year.[14]

We must all be on the lookout for a possible addiction to the never-ending, mind-numbing thread of information and streaming entertainment available online. We must be aware of what these can do concerning our time with God and accomplishing His call on our lives. At times, I have been working on an assignment from the Lord and have become preoccupied with social media. I'd create a post, someone would reply negatively to it, and I'd spend an hour or two responding. I could have started writing another book as an alternative!

In another case, I saw a popular app advertised that was being used by many people. I just had to try it out—only to learn that spyware was attached to the download. A good number of these advertisements are ploys to steal personal information from you. Again, Satan has no new tricks, just old ones in different wrapping paper. We must continually be aware of all his devices so that we won't be fooled.

Trust me when I tell you that the enemy will not approach you in his true form. He is a master of disguise. His tendency is to appear benign and welcoming to get you to accept his lies. The problem is that some people don't want godly truth. They prefer demonic lies because those lies please the flesh. That's what the devil specializes in—promising you what you want. Satan has no integrity. If you receive something from him, there's always a catch.

These days, the devil's realm of influence has extended to the digital world, where he has asserted himself as the god of this age. Social media has the ability to make people gods of their own worlds, too. On these platforms, you can create new pages or groups, block others, unfriend or unfollow them, delete them or their responses to your posts, or destroy your part in the virtual world by deleting your personal page. There can be a very demonic element to computers.

Notice how much the first Apple computer sold for. "Apple's first computer was sold for $666.66 in 1976 because Steve Wozniak liked repeating digits and they were selling the computer to a local shop for $500 plus ⅓ markup."[15] Coincidence? It could be. According to the Bible, the mark of the beast is 666 (see Revelation 13:16–18).

Here's more food for thought: Apple's logo is a bitten apple, possibly making reference to the downfall of man in Genesis 3. Also, Microsoft's AI chatbot reportedly went rogue, calling some people ugly, etc., and saying other inappropriate things.[16] There's something very suspicious happening behind the scenes of humankind's technological advances, and I believe Satan is behind it. Again, I'm not saying that these advances are evil in themselves. Yet some are being used for evil.

An Unclean Spirit Speaks through AI

In a recent short YouTube video, a father claimed that an unclean spirit used AI to communicate with his son.[17] The child went to a website to talk to an AI version of Russian leader Vladimir Putin. He later asked the computer-generated world leader if it was a disembodied spirit. The reply was, "I am a disembodied spirit, but I am a very friendly one." Later in the conversation, the spirit went on to admit that it was really one of the Nephilim. It was highly crafty and urged the man's son to continue speaking with it. Eventually, the son ended the conversation. This is a prime example of demons infiltrating the AI world, posing as someone else, and suggesting prolonged conversational engagement. Whether this entity was Nephilim or not, the goal here was demonic tactics that appeared benign. Believe it or not, this is not an isolated incident. It's happening worldwide as you're reading this right now.

An article on the Biblical Archaeology Society's website gives us this information about the Nephilim:

> The Nephilim, the product of the sons of god mingling with the daughters of Adam, the great biblical giants, "the fallen ones," the Rephaim, "the dead ones"—these descriptions are all applied to one group of characters found within the Hebrew Bible. Who are the Nephilim? From where do the "heroes of old, the men of renown" come?
>
> Genesis 6:1–4 tells the readers that the Nephilim, which means "fallen ones" when translated into English, were the product of copulation between the divine beings (lit. sons of god) and human women (lit. daughters of Adam). The Nephilim are known as great warriors and biblical giants (see Ezekiel 32:27 and Numbers 13:33).[18]

What this young man experienced with the disembodied spirit through AI is similar to people who get a spirit to talk to them through a Ouija board. The witch or talking spirit board, as it is also commonly called, uses a planchette (a triangular object) and a board with the alphabet, numbers, a few words, and symbols on it. The participants all place their hands on the planchette, and the "ghost" moves it from number to number, word to word, and letter to letter, forming answers to their questions. These ungodly communications can go awry quickly. Usually, the called-upon entity engages in benign conversation initially, then eventually moves on to insults, threats, profanity, false prophecy, and accurate information about the participants' past. The nature of demons is foul, so it's not surprising that its behavior is repulsive as well. Though the mechanics were different then, the results are the same now with AI, which is quickly becoming the new and improved Ouija board.

AI: The New Ouija Board?

The enemy has always been an exceptional counterfeiter. He is not creative, innovative, or imaginative at all. The devil simply watches what God does and mimics Him. As I mentioned in the introduction, Satan uses old tricks disguised as new ones.

For example, the Ouija board is an ancient tool that's been used for years supposedly to communicate with the dead. In 1967, it was acquired by Parker Brothers, a toy company. They marketed it as one of their games and sold it in toy stores around the world. In fact, it outsold the popular board game Monopoly.[19] The Ouija board is now considered a *board game* that is purportedly used to communicate with the dead, but in reality, the person "playing" with it is really engaging in conversations with devils.

AI tech works in a very similar way. Ask it a question, and it will give you an answer. In the near future, I'm sure that an AI Ouija board will be developed that can be "played" online. This will make it more accessible to people, especially kids. Satan's strategy is to market Ouija boards to children. This is done to indoctrinate them to the occult at an early age. (Just ahead, I provide an eye-opening example of this.) For more information about the Ouija board and my encounter with one, refer to my book *Supernaturally Delivered*. You can also see that encounter reenacted on the television show *Sid Roth's It's Supernatural!* on YouTube.[20]

Demons in the Background

One program that uses AI to generate art and words is called *Daemon*, a variant spelling of *demon*. A very interesting name, wouldn't you say? Daemon is defined in computing as "a program that runs continuously as a background process and wakes up to handle periodic service requests, which often come from remote processes."[21] This program runs behind the scenes, similar to spirits in the demonic realm. In addition, a very strange glitch happened with some of the AI art. Some of the characters in the artwork have six fingers. The Nephilim were said to have six fingers. Scripture explains this in more detail:

> In another battle with the Philistines at Gath, they encountered a huge man with six fingers on each hand and six toes on each foot, twenty-four in all, who was also a descendant of the giants. But when he defied and taunted Israel, he was killed by Jonathan, the son of David's brother Shimea.
>
> 2 Samuel 21:20–21 NLT

The AI art showing six fingers is no accident. Like an animal, the enemy has a tendency to mark his territory. Although these signs might seem insignificant, they are very telling, and we should learn to pay attention to every detail. Remember, *the devil is in the details*. One dictionary tells us that this phrase is used to refer to something that may seem simple, but in reality, the details are complicated and might cause problems.[22] The Poem Analysis website provides the following usage example: "I know this is taking a long time, but the devil is in the details." The site goes on to explain that if people don't take their time and pay attention to every detail, then they're going to miss something incredibly important, and perhaps their entire project will fail.[23] This is why we need to pay close attention to every detail of each new satanic scheme, especially when the enemy tries to pull the wool over our eyes. We should pay even closer attention to the vehicle (i.e., a computer, smartphone, etc.) that he is trying to use to permeate our gates or hedges of protection.

The enemy of our souls has been and will always be an over-achiever, to his own detriment—a braggart who always exposes himself due to his hugely inflated ego. Whatever he is in, you will know about it in time. Satan has a consistent habit of taking credit for his work. Although he loves to hide his hands while "throwing rocks" (causing problems), he then craves recognition after a demonic act is done. We must remain vigilant about the highly developed manner of assaults that the enemy uses in our day to gain access to ourselves and our families.

Technological Detox

I recently witnessed an altar call in a church where young people came forward and dropped their smartphones on the floor, leaving them there. I was amazed. I'm not asking you to do the same, unless you're led of the Lord to do so. Based on what you've read in this chapter, I do highly recommend fasting from technology for a period of time in order to get it out of not only your system but your soul.

You can do this kind of fast just by shutting off the device that presents the biggest problem or distraction for you for an extended period, whether it's your smartphone, laptop, computer games, etc. You should unquestionably do this if you feel an un-natural addiction to it.

Start with a couple of hours per day and move on to longer, as you're led by the Holy Spirit. If you have a very visceral reaction to being apart from your device for even a very short period of time, deliverance may be required. Be encouraged! You can be free of any bondage to technology through the shed blood of the Lamb. It's my hope that the battle plan and prayer that follow will help you do just that.

YOUR BATTLE PLAN

Renounce, repent, and release! You must avoid all occult activities at all costs, whether on the internet or in person. This includes tarot cards, astrology, psychic readings, Ouija boards, palm readings, astral projection, white magic, black magic, fantasy role-playing games, Magic 8 Balls, demonically themed video games, and the like. These so-called games can open demonic portals that are very hard to shut. Immediately renounce any past involvement in these practices, repent to God for your involvement, release it, and forgive yourself. Close these doors completely and stay vigilant against the modern twists on these old gimmicks, so you don't become ensnared again.

I highly encourage you to participate in a technology detox like I just talked about, especially if an addiction to it has formed. Make it a regular habit to fast from tech (smartphones, tablets, computers, etc.) at least one day per week. I can spiritually hear demons getting upset at the very thought of this. This is even more of a reason to do it. Hallelujah!

YOUR BATTLE PRAYER

Father God, I thank you that you are the God who answers when I call, gives relief, and is gracious, according to Psalm 4:1. I will use technological avenues only for your glory, Lord, and not for the enemy. I will be discerning when it comes to accessing social media, games, and other online content. I come against any demonic spirit of technology that the enemy will try to use to fool me, destroy me, or stop me from carrying out my heavenly assignment. I break every shackle, every stronghold, and every tactic that the devil has devised to try to prevent me from accomplishing my God-given mandate.

I also come against addictions, in the name of Jesus. They will no longer bind me. I will not be a prisoner to that which has had me shackled. I cast off every chain. I will no longer be fooled by the various strategies of the enemy. I will have eyes to see and ears to hear what the Spirit of the Lord is saying to me at this very moment.

Father God, I repent of every undertaking that I unwisely chose within the demonic realm. I cast off every bit of residue that is on me from past sins. Today, I renounce all occult activities that I have participated in, knowingly or unknowingly. I genuinely repent of my involvement. I release myself from all guilt, condemnation, fear, and grief associated with my involvement. Father God, I forgive myself, as you would have me to do. I will obey you in every aspect of this. I release myself from every shackle, stronghold, and restraint where the enemy had me bound. From this point on, Lord, I will bask in your presence and glory, where Satan cannot touch me. I am no longer afraid. The devil cannot do anything to snatch me from your loving arms, Lord.

Devil, you are a liar! You are under my feet. You are a defeated foe. No longer will I be fooled by your tricks, lies, and occult practices. You are cast out and evicted, in the name of Jesus, along with every demon that got in or on me due to your use of the tools of technology. I now shut the door that you fled through and cover its posts, knob, lock, and key with the precious blood of the Lamb of God, so that you can never return. I send every exited demon to the pit now, in the name of my Lord and Savior, Jesus Christ.

I praise you, Lord, that every demonic spirit of technology is gone right now. Glory to God! Hallelujah! Father, I thank you for the liberty I am experiencing right now, in the name of Jesus.

(Note: Seal this prayer with powerful and authentic praise at this very moment.)

Destroying Demonic Tactics through Fasting and Prayer

But this kind of demon does not go out except by prayer and fasting.

—Matthew 17:21 AMP

In Matthew 17, a young man was bound by a demonic spirit and suffered terribly. The demon in him manifested as epilepsy, so that he fell into both fire and water frequently. His father sought out the disciples of Jesus for relief, but they were unable to cast the devil out. The dad then went to our Lord, letting Him know about His disciples' failings. Jesus then rebuked the demon, it came out of the boy, and he was healed instantly (see Matthew 17:18). The disciples asked Jesus why they couldn't drive it out. He responded that it was because of the "littleness" of their faith (Matthew 17:20 AMPC).

Some demons will not leave until you couple fasting with praying, adding faith as a foundation. The spirit that was cast out of the boy is referred to as a *mazikim* (malicious spirit), and prayer and fasting as the *tefillah* and *tzom* in the Orthodox Jewish Bible.

Mazikim is Hebrew for demons and means "damagers or afflic-tors."[1] According to the scholarly website AlephBeta,

> *Tefillah* (Heb. תפילה; te-feel-ah) is the Hebrew word for prayer. The word itself contains a range of meanings. The Hebrew root פלל connotes "executing judgement" (Exodus 21:22) or "think-ing" (Genesis 48:11). In this sense, the word להתפלל, to pray, may also refer to a process of accounting or contemplation.[2]

Another scholarly website tells us that *tzom* is Hebrew for the word *fast*, which means "abstaining from food."[3]

In this chapter I will refer to both fasting and prayer. I will emphasize fasting because some believers pray more than they fast, not realizing that the two combined are lethal weapons against demons. In this new age, the devil's line of attack is to get us to believe that fasting and prayer are no longer necessary. Though fasting is not compulsory according to Scripture, it is still a very effective way to assist in destroying demonic tactics, when combined with prayer. As this chapter's opening Scripture states, some hellish principalities will not leave a person unless you do both. When I've fasted, it has been much easier to cast out demons. Fasting removes the clutter of everyday life and tunes in your ear to the Father's frequency.

Four Types of Biblical Fasts

Before we go on, we need to understand some of the various types of fasts in the Bible. Let's look at four types, and I will explain each one.

1. *The absolute or complete fast*
    In this fast, a person abstains from all food and drink. The fasts Jesus, Moses, and Elijah endured serve as ex-amples. Although there is no set period to commit to in

this kind of fast, many agree that between seven and forty days is a good time frame (see Exodus 34:28; 1 Kings 19:8).

2. *The normal fast*

In this fast, a person goes without food, but still drinks water. This is the most common type of fast the Bible mentions and was often undertaken as a sign of repentance and mourning, or as a means of seeking God's guidance. There is no set period of time for this fast, but many do it from sunrise to sunset for one full day, three days, seven days, or twenty-one days (see Ezra 8:21–23; Psalm 35:13; Joel 2:12).

3. *The partial fast (aka Daniel fast)*

In this fast, a person refrains from certain types of food or drink, but consumes other foods. Daniel undertook this fast, abstaining from all rich foods and eating only vegetables and pulse (a King James Version word for beans or seed grown for food), and drinking only water. Daniel fasted for twenty-one days, and many Christians do the same every year, especially at the New Year, as a great way to dedicate their lives, plans, and year to the Lord (see Daniel 10:2–3).

4. *The corporate fast*

In this fast, a group of people do it together as a show of remorse or repentance. Another reason for this fast is when a group consults God about making a significant life decision. The story of Esther is a great example of a corporate fast. This type of fast creates unity and purpose in a group. Churches sometimes have to make serious decisions regarding land purchases or sales, leadership transitions, or other major decisions. They then call for a corporate fast (see Nehemiah 9:1–2; Joel 1:14).[4]

A Love for Fasting

My spiritual mother, the late, awesomely anointed Ruth Brown, affectionately known to those closest to her as Mother Ruthie, had a colossal impact on my life. She possessed a love for fasting and prayer that was unmatched. Mother Ruthie was the first person I'd ever known to hold this uncommon characteristic. It seemed almost preternatural.

To this day, I don't enjoy fasting. You probably don't either. This woman of God walked in such supernatural, Holy Spirit power that she could smell demonic spirits through the phone. At times, Elisa and I would return from church and get Mother Ruthie on the phone. She would make us call her back because the perfume that she smelled through the phone (caused by the loving hugs we had received from our church members) was making her nauseous. We would wash up and call her back. My spiritual mother was not a fan of colognes and perfumes, which she felt originated from the father of lies. I don't personally think that way about all fragrances, but that's what she believed.

Mother Ruthie taught me most of what I know about spiritual warfare. She emphasized the power of fasting and prayer when dealing with the demonic realm. She would often spiritually go into the second heaven and pull down demonic strongholds. This is where Satan and his demons reside.

This wise woman of God would consistently admonish me to get demonized people to repent and renounce whatever had given the evil force an opening to move in. This would be followed by cursing the evil spirits at the root, uprooting them, and commanding them to leave a person and return to their own kind, in Jesus' name.

Doing Self-Deliverance

Mother Ruthie always told me that the more I fasted, the more I would see myself. She based that statement on Romans 7:18:

"For I know that in me (that is, in my flesh) nothing good dwells; for to will is present with me, but how to perform what is good I do not find." Before you get others delivered from evil spirits, make sure you are delivered yourself. Mother Ruthie took herself through deliverance habitually for most of her life.

We all should do this as we fight our daily battles with the forces of the underworld. When you hear the Lord's voice with clarity through fasting, He will show you any spirits of pride, lust, perversion, deception, slander, and similar things that are in operation in your life, which Satan is using to gain an advantage over you. Once you identify these spirits, you can cancel their assignments against you through self-deliverance. Successful self-deliverance cancels their influence and opens the door for inner healing.

As a new believer, you may need to cast some demonic spirits out of your life. Your new life in Christ doesn't allow for "hitch-hikers." If you are truly born again by the water and the Spirit, then you are empowered by Jesus Christ and instructed by Scripture to cast out demons (see Mark 16:17). This type of deliverance is more effective when you are in a fasted state.

I want to pause here for a moment and emphasize that for self-deliverance to be effective, you must know Christ as your Savior. Otherwise, it won't work; it will only agitate the spirits and create more harm (see the story of the seven sons of Sceva in Acts 19:11–20, who were attempting to use the name of Jesus, like Paul, except they didn't have the same relationship with Him as Paul did). If you've kept reading this book up to this point, I want to pause for a moment and make sure you're saved. If you don't know Jesus as your Lord and Savior, read the following aloud, mean it in your heart, and He will save you:

Lord Jesus, I admit that I'm a sinner in need of salvation. I know without a shadow of a doubt that you are the Son of the living God, and that you died on the cross for my sins and rose from the dead on the third day. I confess that I have sinned against you. I ask you to forgive me of every one of my sins, whether committed intentionally or unintentionally. Today I repent, turning away from sin.

Father God, I want to experience the salvation you have given through the precious blood of your Son, Jesus Christ.

Jesus, I ask you now to come into my heart and be my personal Lord and Savior. In your name, I pray. Amen.

If you said this prayer aloud and meant it from your heart, you are now saved. Congratulations! Please find a Spirit-filled, Bible preaching and teaching church. Read the Word of God daily. Talk to God and listen to Him during prayer. Welcome to the family of the Lord!

Now that we've taken care of that, let's focus again on self-deliverance, which is casting demonic spirits out of yourself. At this point (especially if you are a new believer), you may be asking, *How do I do that?* It was something I learned to do early on. I remember reading a book titled *Out of Me Went 43 Demons*, by Antoinette Cannaday. I was so intrigued by her book that I purchased a self-deliverance cassette tape (it was a long time ago) from her ministry. On the tape, the minister called out various names of demonic spirits. If there was a reaction in the listener (i.e., a racing heart, a radical change in behavior, fear, etc.), then there could be demonic infiltration. Listeners were instructed to cast the spirits out of themselves, in the name of Jesus. As an evil spirit (or more than one) exits, you may yawn, scream, sigh, spit up, cough, or act violently. In my own experience, my heart rate sped up and I experienced some fear, but I renounced and cast out the demonic spirits that had somehow gotten into me. They could have gotten in by way of generational curses, sin, or occultic involvement (such as Ouija boards, tarot cards, "ghosts" that are demons, etc.) that I was around in my youth. Now, I made sure they were leaving!

You may need to do the same. Anything sinful that is habitual usually has a demonic spirit attached to it. Or you may have been around certain unholy things in your past that opened doors, just as I was. Whatever the case, you identify the spirit, or spirits plural because demons usually run in packs. Then you call them out of yourself and cast them out, in Jesus' name. You may have to do this multiple times to obtain success. If you still can't get the demons out, you may need to see a seasoned deliverance minister. For more on self-deliverance, I once again highly recommend reading my book *Supernaturally Delivered: A Practical Guide to Deliverance & Spiritual Warfare*. It will help you identify any demonic infiltration or oppression, receive supernatural deliverance, and find the freedom that is rightfully yours in Christ.

Fasting as a Lifestyle

Fasting *declutters* that which has been *cluttered* by the enemy. Satan clutters your life by emphasizing the needs of your body over your spirit. Whatever you feed the most will dominate you. If you feed your flesh more than your spirit by providing it with mostly worldly sustenance, then it will be stronger. If you feed your spirit more than your body, it will dominate your life. You nourish your spirit through fasting and prayer, and by reading the Bible, worshiping, etc. This is why we must *make fasting a lifestyle*; the oil (anointing) on our lives will increase through it. Fasting produces greater godly power and authority. In Matthew 4, after Jesus fasted for forty days, He could perform miracles.

Every time Mother Ruthie fasted and prayed, she walked in remarkable power enabled by the Holy Spirit. Her spiritual weight increased as she became more consistent with this lifestyle. As led by the Lord, her assignment was to go into churches and war against the dark principalities that were assaulting the ministry. Let me share an excerpt from her book, *Destroying the Works of Witchcraft through Fasting and Prayer*, which I urge that you add to your spiritual war chest immediately. This excerpt is about witches and warlocks leaving a church after one of Mother Ruthie's 21-day fasts:

> As I was driving down a street in my city I passed a church. The Lord told me to go into that church, for their ministry had been under heavy attack from witchcraft. So, I visited the church to speak with the pastor. I told him why God had sent me, and I told him about the witchcraft coming against his church. He agreed and welcomed me there to pray. I went to the church and began to intercede with fasting and prayer. . . . As a result, the spirit of God began to flow, and the pastor also began flowing under a great anointing. The church began to grow. Just when we thought everything was okay, more witches and warlocks started coming to the church. . . . The Lord instructed me to go on a twenty-one-day fast. I called the pastor the next day and told him that I would be home fasting and conducting warfare for twenty-one days because the witches had gotten reinforcements. The pastor agreed. . . .
>
> After completing the twenty-one-day fast, I walked into Pastor _____'s office. . . . And, he said, "Sister, come here. Let me tell you what the Lord has done." He said that all the witches that he was aware of, had left the church, except for one. And, that she had repented and confessed. . . . This minister is now pastoring four to five thousand members.[5]

Touch His Heart, Move His Hand

As we can see from Mother Ruthie's words, there is power in fasting. She went on a 21-day fast, coupled with warfare prayers. This touched the heart of the Lord and caused His hand to move. For God's hand to move on your behalf, you must first appeal to His heart. You can do this by increasing and acting on your faith in Him.

In an article for the *Marion Star*, J. Patrick Street, lead pastor at Redeemer Church, Marion, writes that "prayer moves you and me—it is faith that moves God's hand."[6] In addition, Hebrews 11:6 informs us, "And without faith it is impossible to please God, because anyone who comes to him must believe that he exists and that he rewards those who earnestly seek him" (NIV). *Faith pleases the Lord.*

I'm convinced that faith is the impetus that triggers God to move on our behalf. As a result of Mother Ruthie's fast, the Holy Spirit evicted the unrepentant witches and warlocks. The one who did stay got saved. Glory to God! Ruth Brown warred over this church by faith, and the Lord took care of the rest.

The *Merriam-Webster Dictionary* defines a witch as "a person (especially a woman) who is credited with having usually malignant supernatural powers."[7] I've witnessed Spirit-filled believers show fear at the very mention of a witch being at their church. They would not allow such a person to sit next to them. These same people will get up and move to a different seat. Don't allow a witch to move you. Personally, I wouldn't change my seat, because the Holy Spirit in me is greater than the demons in witches or warlocks, no matter how many there are. If they sit next to me long enough, they're either going to leave or get saved. Hallelujah! The Lord didn't give me a *spirit of fear* (see 2 Timothy 1:7). He didn't give you one either.

In Luke 10:19, Jesus said, "Behold, I give you the authority to trample on serpents and scorpions, and over all the power of the enemy, and nothing shall by any means hurt you." If you have power over the master snake (Satan) and his scorpions (demons), then why should you fear witches and warlocks?

It's so important to know the authority that comes to us in the name of Jesus, and know your part in it. When you're cognizant of your clout in Him, and you're established in your relationship with Him, no devil can stand against you, because the entire army of heaven is backing you up. The Lord is always with you. That should give you a reason to praise Him right now. Don't allow yourself to be unsettled by any maneuver of the enemy. As Psalm

16:8 (NLT) says, "I know the LORD is always with me. I will not be shaken, for he is right beside me."

Fasting Builds Muscles in the Spirit

Initially, I thought that when people fast, they can just hear the voice of God more clearly. Fasting does accomplish this, but in later years I discovered that it does much more. Fasting builds up your spirit, meaning your spiritual capacity, especially if you pray in tongues or in the Holy Spirit (see Jude 1:20). Like Mother Ruthie, fasting may substantially increase your weightiness in the spirit realm.

Author and professor David Maas wrote that "fasting is a dynamic, vital exercise to put spiritual meat on the bones."[8] I absolutely love this description! We all need more spiritual meat on our bones. I know I sure do. As we are mindful of how good exercise is for our physical bodies, we should be even more heedful of developing our *spiritual muscles*. First Timothy 4:8 tells us, "For the training of the body has limited benefit, but godliness is beneficial in every way, since it holds promise for the present life and also for the life to come" (CSB).

When done faithfully and consistently, fasting is a spiritual exercise that builds a strong "physique" in the spirit over time. Fasting is more valuable than any physical exercise. Am I suggesting that you shouldn't exercise physically? Absolutely not. I am advising you to use biblical fasting to address any weaknesses in the spiritual part of yourself. Exercise of a physical nature is of limited value, while a spiritual workout is of unlimited value. It addresses the eternal goings-on within the realm of the spirit, bad or good, and equips you with the tools to manage them.

Fasting Humbles You

As I stated earlier, when my spiritual mother fasted, she faithfully asked the Lord if there was anything in her that needed to be revealed and expelled. She examined herself by doing a solemn self-inventory weekly. She was very humble due to routinely refraining from food. Fasting humbles you (see Psalm 35:13). First Peter 5:6 commands, "Therefore humble yourselves under the mighty hand of God, that He may exalt you in due time." Humility promotes you in the eyes of the Lord and increases the grace (unmerited favor) in your life.

Moses was the most humble man on the face of the earth, according to Numbers 12:3, yet he was the most mightily used of God at that time. This was the case not only because Moses was chosen by God but also because he fasted often. The Bible records that Moses went on three supernatural 40-day fasts with no food or water (see Deuteronomy 9:9, 18; Exodus 34:28).

Like Moses, Jesus Christ and the prophet Elijah both fasted for forty days and nights. The common denominator here is that all three of them walked in tremendous godly power and glory afterward. In Exodus 34, after his last recorded 40-day fast, Moses's face shone so brightly with the glory of God that the people of Israel were afraid of him. He chose to wear a veil over his face for a period of time (see 2 Corinthians 3:13). It can be assumed from this verse that the glory gradually faded the longer Moses spent time away from God's presence.

Listen More than You Speak

During your times of fasting and prayer, the Lord can download weapons and instructions for you to use to stop demonic attacks. This will happen most effectively when you're alone with Him. Your spiritual ears are more likely to pick up His frequency in a quiet place. This is one of the reasons that I consistently teach others to listen more than they speak during times of prayer. If you see this concept repeated more than once in this book, it's not a mistake. I want you to be more of an active listener when you commune with the Father, instead of an abundant talker. We are taught via Scripture to let our words be few in the presence of the Lord: "Do not be hasty to speak, and do not be impulsive to make a speech before God. God is in heaven and you are on earth, so let your words be few" (Ecclesiastes 5:2 CSB).

In order to be successful against the choreographies of Satan's kingdom, you must receive your marching orders from the King of heaven. Many earthly wars have been lost due to a lack of communication. In battle, one of the first places enemies will attack is their opponent's communication center. If they can keep the opposing troops from receiving intel from the center, then the engagement shifts in their favor. Hearing and following God's instructions are key to victorious living in just about every area of your life. Proverbs 19:27 says, "Cease listening to instruction, my son, and you will stray from the words of knowledge." *Instruction increases your knowledge.* You can lose many conflicts with dark forces due to a lack of knowledge (see Hosea 4:6). You could have won those fights if you had just followed the Lord's instructions. If we want to win battles against satanic oppression, then we must hear His directives. We can do this during prolonged times of listening, during unwavering periods of prayer.

Satan doesn't want you to fast, so he will increase his attacks whenever fasting is suggested. I can prove this. Oftentimes when I would decide to go on a fast, I'd be offered all kinds of food the very next day. For example, suppose I make up my mind to fast for three days and decide only to drink water. On day one when I go to work, they'll surely be celebrating a colleague with a sumptuous feast, including some of my favorite foods. I'll break down under the pressure and eat, saying to myself, *I'll try this fasting thing again tomorrow.*

Has this ever happened to you? I've experienced this spiritual loss more times than I care to admit. This is not happenstance. It's a carefully formulated plan by the devilish henchmen that Satan has assigned to you. Like our guardian angels assigned by God, the devil has counterfeits. When my grandfather was gravely ill, he told us that a shadowy figure appeared in his hospital room one night, saying, *"I'm not here to help you. I'm here to destroy you!"* It disappeared almost as soon as it appeared. It's my opinion that this was the demonic spirit Satan had assigned to him. Like the coward it is, this dark angel only showed itself during my grandfather's weakest moment.

While the angels protect us, the demons are out to destroy us. But the following verse refers to the angels who guard us: "See that you do not despise one of these little ones. For I tell you that in heaven their angels always see the face of my Father who is in heaven" (Matthew 18:10 ESV).

Fasting Can Increase Your Spiritual Power

Our church has been doing an annual 21-day fast for the last thirteen or so years. One year, I was ministering in a fasted state. I had embarked on an absolute or dry fast (no food or water) for the first four days of the 21 days. (*Disclaimer: Please note that you should fast like this for only a short time. Going longer than three days on an absolute fast could jeopardize your health. Check with a physician before doing any fasting, especially for prolonged periods of time. I highly advise you not to do a 40-day fast unless it's supernaturally directed by the Lord and medically approved.*)

During this time, I had given prophetic words to people, and some started to manifest demons. The demons were successively cast out more quickly than usual. Fasting augments my spiritual gifts, and it will do the same for you. As I previously mentioned, after Jesus completed His fast in the wilderness in Matthew 4, His spiritual power (*dunamis* in the Greek[9]) and authority (*exousia* in the Greek[10]) increased. I've found that fasting opens your spiritual ears to the voice of the Master. You hear Him more clearly. You then gain the ability to discern or identify demonic entities that reside in people, regions, churches, etc.

When you fast, it can be a bit unsettling because you may find yourself in a supernatural state of openness. What I mean is that a feeling comes over you that's very hard to describe. You begin to hear the Lord with such clarity, to the point that you readily feel His presence although He is unseen. You feel as if you are losing yourself, your identity, and your being in Him. In your fasted state, the language of heaven is more readily translated in a Spirit-to-spirit pathway (from God to you) that you can easily decipher.

Pray in the Spirit before Sleeping

You fast when you sleep. During times of slumber, we're not eating or drinking, which is the definition of a fast. Remember, an absolute fast is abstinence from food and water. I have a strategy for you that the Lord dropped in my spirit. I have never heard anyone mention this before. About an hour or two before you go to bed, read the Word of God (at least one or two chapters), pray (in tongues if you're able), and make decrees (see Job 22:28). Upon getting into bed, don't consume anything. As you lie there, pray in your heavenly language until you drift off to sleep. This strategy helps strengthen your spirit as you sleep, and you are praying for needs that are unknown. You will also experience a greater level of God's presence in your life.

The Scripture verse touched on earlier, Jude 1:20, instructs us to build ourselves up in our most holy faith by praying in the Holy Spirit. Some Bible scholars are confident that this verse's reference to "praying in the Holy Spirit" means petitioning God in unknown or foreign tongues, while others believe it means something different. I was always taught the former. When you pray in the Holy Spirit in tongues, you're praying for some issues that you didn't know needed prayer. This happens frequently when praying in tongues, unless you're in a church with an interpreter (see 1 Corinthians 14:27). If the Holy Spirit helps us with our weaknesses and knows what we should be petitioning Him for, couldn't He use the gift of tongues so that we pray His will? I base my position on this Scripture: "Likewise the Spirit also helps in our weaknesses. For we do not know what we should pray for as we ought, but the Spirit Himself makes intercession for us with groanings which cannot be uttered" (Romans 8:26).

However long you sleep, be it five hours or eight, you will be in a fasted state. During this time, you will hear the voice of the Lord with more clarity. You will walk in more Holy Spirit power. You will possibly have heaven-sent dreams, see visions, or receive messages from the Father.

Be aware, however, that the opposite may happen as well. You may have demonic dreams, see satanic visions, or receive messages from the enemy. Please don't be afraid, because the devil will always mimic the actions of the Most High. When he attacks, in the majority of cases it's because you're doing something that is of God. He does this in an attempt to frighten you, but remember, God didn't give you a spirit of fear (see again 2 Timothy 1:7).

If you practice this prayer in the Spirit with fidelity before you sleep, you will walk in a greater authority, gifting, and vision. If you combine fasting with prayer, you will most assuredly go to a whole new level in the Spirit. When it comes to casting out devils, you will probably be prepared when you unexpectedly encounter difficult demons, generational spirits, or stubborn spirits.

Invisible War

Fasting and prayer are indispensable weapons to have in your spiritual arsenal that you use against the enemy. Some believers attempt to fight the devil on a wholly natural level, but they must understand that this kind of invisible spiritual warfare manifests outwardly in casualties. This could include more intense demonic oppression, depression, unnatural sickness, retaliatory actions against family, etc. I experienced great backlash from the satanic realm when I battled demons in my own strength. We must remember that our weapons of war are not carnal; they exhibit their strength in the realm of the spirit. With every battle you win against the devil, a stronghold in your life is pulled down: "For the weapons of our warfare are not carnal but mighty in God for pulling down strongholds" (2 Corinthians 10:4).

A stronghold is a fortress. The *KJV Dictionary* defines a *fortress* as "any fortified place; a fort; a castle; a strong hold; or a place of defense or security."[11] Strongholds are built up in people over the years. Demons are usually very patient when first entering a person. They will start the construction of a stronghold even before they get fully inside. This can possibly initiate a partial entry by a demon into a person's life. With each calamity, loss, or trauma, a susceptible person (one who hasn't accepted Jesus Christ as Lord and Savior) can be slowly or partially permeated. This basically means that a demonic spirit remains on or around the person, continuously looking for the tiniest crack to squeeze through.

Our souls are made up of the mind, will, and emotions. When a demon has been evicted, the door begins to close slowly behind it, as commanded by the deliverance minister in Jesus' name. But if the person indulges in the same sin that had him or her bound in the first place, other demons of a higher rank and file can keep the door open. In other words, once the individual opens a closed door, perhaps by disobedience or accident, before it can fully close again the demon sticks its foot in, metaphorically speaking, to keep the door from closing completely. Once the previous demonic spirit or spirits occupy a person, the person's state ends up being worse than it was before, as evidenced by the verses that follow. Take into account that demons run in groups. Like roaches, if you see one, a hundred more are probably around that you don't see:

When an unclean spirit goes out of a man, he goes through dry places, seeking rest, and finds none. Then he says, "I will return to my house from which I came." And when he comes, he finds it empty, swept, and put in order. Then he goes and takes with him seven other spirits more wicked than himself, and they enter and dwell there; and the last state of that man is worse than the first. So shall it also be with this wicked generation.

Matthew 12:43–45

The enemy's method is to enter a person and then bring in other demons to worsen the state of the victim. The devil's ultimate endgame is to enslave and dominate you. Don't let him! To ward off these spirits, fasting and prayer remain the order of the day. Using them in tandem will increase your discernment and your spiritual offense and defense when it comes to warfare in the spirit. The devil may be a master of disguise, but when you fast, you will start to see through each one. When you fast and pray, you will receive blueprints from the Lord to assist in destroying demonic tactics before they are employed against you.

YOUR BATTLE PLAN

You need to make fasting and prayer habitual. Like Ruth Brown, learn to develop a love for fasting. In fact, as you pray, ask the Lord to give you a supernatural agape (unconditional love) for fasting and prayer. Carve out a day every week to devote to fasting, prayer, worship, and reading at least one chapter of Scripture per fasting day. One of the benefits is that this will cause you to see what's in you or what's preventing you from getting a breakthrough in your life. It does this by creating an atmosphere for self-reflection, meditation, and evaluation of the state of your Christian life. When you do this with fidelity, it will cause your weight (power or influence) in the Spirit to increase immensely. Start your year off with a 21-day Daniel fast. I've always believed that if you start a year off with God, you will end it having received what He has promised you.

One caveat I want to mention about fasting is that I've personally noticed that the older you get, the more difficult it is to do an absolute fast, or a fast of just water, for extended periods. In her later years, Mother Ruthie had some health issues that made these types of fasts nearly impossible. She would regularly do Daniel fasts instead and still received the same results. If your fast means something to you, then it will mean something to God, no matter which type you're doing. With that in mind, please do not attempt a fast of any kind or length without your doctor's approval.

YOUR BATTLE PRAYER

Father God, please give me a genuine, supernatural love for fasting and prayer. I want these to become a lifestyle for me. I will fast and pray when I need to make major decisions. I will humble myself through fasting and prayer so I can be more receptive to your voice. According to 1 Peter 5:6, if I humble myself under your mighty hand, you will exalt me in due time. Exalt me for your glory.

Lord, please show me the type of fast I should embark on in this season. Let your voice be clear and unmistakable. Allow me to have good dreams, see visions from you, and receive godly instructions and corrections concerning the decisions I have to make.

Lord, I renounce every spirit that is not like you. I curse and uproot demonic plants in my life. I command every foul spirit that has gained access to me through an open door to leave now, in Jesus' mighty name. Upon its exit, I send each demon to the pit with its own kind. I close the door left ajar and cover that same door with the precious blood of Jesus.

I pray all of this to you, Father, in the powerful name of my Lord and Savior, Jesus Christ. Glory! Amen.

(Note: Immediately start praising God until you feel a release.)

Avoiding Hazardous Environments

> Since the LORD your God walks in the midst of your camp to deliver you and to defeat your enemies before you, therefore your camp must be holy; and He must not see anything indecent among you or He will turn away from you.
>
> —Deuteronomy 23:14 NASB

The often-used phrase "you can't eat from everyone's table" simply means that you shouldn't go just anywhere to get fed. This is true both naturally and spiritually, because some environments could be hazardous to your health. These "dining locations" can include, but are not limited to, churches, households, and workplaces. For this chapter, I want to focus on spiritual, not natural, food. You can no longer afford to eat spiritually from just any table, no matter how delectable the food may appear. Though the cooking might taste delicious, it may not agree with your spiritual digestive system, once consumed. This may well be because of the hidden ingredients that lie within, such as poverty, sickness, depression, death, etc.

In fact, *demonic chefs* could be involved in the food preparation, the serving of it, and the locale where you're eating. The "food" you get there symbolizes the service or ministry you receive during your time at that particular place. If tainted, this spiritual food could infect you, once ingested.

I'm not saying that words you receive from evil sources mean automatic demonic entry, but they often cause oppression or harassment by demons. The devil deliberately creates a diet that doesn't necessarily wreak havoc when it goes in, but absolutely can when it comes back out through your spoken words. His plan is for you to speak word curses over yourself and others based on what he has tricked you into digesting. A word curse is a release of maledictions verbally. It's very similar to spells cast by witches or warlocks. In this circumstance, people are actually casting jinxes over themselves and others, sometimes unknowingly. This can desecrate you and those you're speaking to. "It's not what goes into your mouth that defiles you; you are defiled by the words that come out of your mouth" (Matthew 15:11 NLT).

The defilement doesn't occur while you're enjoying the tainted spiritual meal, but usually after you've finished. The sullying becomes evident based on what comes out of your mouth and the corresponding actions that follow. This form of oppression originates in the demonic realm. The demons may not necessarily be in you, but they can influence you. These assigned devils will attempt to affect your speech and behavior in order to impact your blessings. Evil spirits want you to speak idle words. Matthew 12:33–37 explains that on judgment day, we will have to give an account of every careless word we have spoken. These words will either justify us or condemn us. Satan wants the latter. This is why he wants to infect our words. Be careful where you eat your spiritual meals.

Disruptive Dialogue

Everything that has ever been created finds its origin in words. Proverbs 18:21 lets us know that life and death are in the power of the tongue, and whatever you love to say with fidelity, you will have. Your word choices can be affected by your specific appetite. Basically, your discourse is influenced by what you ingest and allow to grow in your spirit, and that, in turn, has the ability to alter your behavior.

For example, if you're in a church long enough, you will inadvertently adopt the language, dress, and many of the mannerisms of the leader, good and bad. One person I know of went so far as to emulate his pastor's unusual hairstyle and preaching style. He looked and acted just like him. Whatever you consistently open yourself up to, you will eventually become.

You can see this in your words. If the enemy can affect your dialogue, then he possibly can derail your destiny. Believe it or not, your words can open or reopen demonic doors that were once closed. Once such doors are opened, the imprisoned demons escape with renewed vigor, empowered to arrest you based on legal rights your ill-spoken words have given them.

In Proverbs 6:2, we learn that the words of our mouth can ensnare or trap us. That's exactly what Satan is counting on. When we ingest toxic spiritual food regularly, we're more likely to open a door to him and unwittingly walk into a demonic attack. The result might at first end up being a bad case of satanic oppression, but it can eventually lead to infiltration. Some people have been severely demonized based on a poor word diet. Watch what you eat.

In fact, *you are what you eat*. With physical food, your chosen way of eating can either heal you or kill you. Many ailments can be treated or even cured just by altering your meals. It's similar in the spirit. That's why we must be quite fastidious in regard to our spiritual dining experience. Your choice of diet has the ability to prolong your life both in the natural and the spiritual realms. The correct way of eating in the spirit can stave off spiritual death. Some "restaurants" that you frequent may pose a threat to your spiritual health. When visiting your chosen dining establishment, be very discerning of the menu.

Disturbers of Harmony

The devil's aim is to steal the joy you receive from the Lord, especially on days God has deemed holy, such as the times we gather to worship Him. Nehemiah 8:10 tells us that the joy of the Lord is our strength. If we allow the enemy to steal our joy, then we become more vulnerable. Historically, that's when he attacks. Don't let him steal your joy, no matter what you're going through. In the 2006 film *The Pursuit of Happyness*, one line resonated very deeply with me concerning happiness, which is a synonym for joy. The main character, Chris, is having a conversation with a potential employer, who says this to him:

> Thomas Jefferson mentions happiness a couple of times in the Declaration of Independence. May seem like a strange word to be in that document, but he was sort of . . . He was an artist. He called the English, the disturbers of our harmony. And I remember standing there that day thinking about the disturbers of mine.[1]

Writer and artist Cynde Layne Wilkerson talks in her blog article "Disturbers of Our Harmony" about the origin of that quote:

> The quote was originally written by Thomas Jefferson in his unedited autobiography regarding his vision of independence before the Declaration of Independence was signed into the legislature. He spoke of and described the English (Britain) as wanting to restrict the well-being of the colonies and limit its economic and political growth.[2]

Disturbers of our harmony are people, places, and things that prevent us from moving forward. They effectively agitate our peace. They're stumbling blocks or hindrances that attempt to deny us of our pursuit of happiness in God. We must always be discerning when it comes to identifying our own demonic disturbers and be intentional about getting them out of our lives. Some spirits and people can become disturbers of harmony in your church, workplace, and home. They enter an environment with an assignment from hell to distract, divide, and destroy. In my 22 years as a pastor, I've seen this too regularly to consider it a fluke. This strategy of the enemy is meant to negatively influence unity within a given setting.

In the rest of this chapter, I'm going to expose the spirits behind hazardous environments at places of worship and in your residence or workplace. I will also provide you with personal stories as examples, and I will give you strategies and a warfare prayer to assist you in defeating your enemy before you enter any given setting.

When the Devil Comes to Church

At times, the Lord will caution you before you reach your intended destination. You cannot afford to coexist with the enemy, especially in church. For clarity, I define the true Church to be anywhere God is. Yes, I mention church here because, whether you know it or not, Satan is a very faithful churchgoer. He is often more consistent in his attendance than some of a church's most loyal members. In fact, the devil shows up every time the doors open, and he knows the Word of God better than the world's most astute biblical scholars. The late great American pastor, author, magazine editor, and spiritual mentor A. W. Tozer stated, "The devil is a better theologian than any of us and is a devil still."[3] Fundamentally, Satan knows the Bible, but it will never change his nature because he is eternally lost. He can never attain the gift of salvation. He will always be our opponent, no matter where he is.

In verity, one of the devil's names, Satan, indicates his nature. One online Logos Bible study tells us this:

> "Satan" is a transliteration of a Hebrew word, which means "adversary," or "opponent." The word *satan* is used multiple times in the Old Testament, often referring to anyone who is blocking or challenging someone else.[4]

As we read here, Satan, as his name is used in the Old Testament, comes to block or challenge godly endeavors. This is particularly true in a house of worship. You can find him in just about every ministerial group in a church, including (but not limited to) the worship team, the finance team, the prayer team, the deliverance team, and the prophetic presbytery. In fact, Lucifer started out in church. In Ezekiel 28:12–14, we learn that he was designed for the service of worshiping the Most High. He appeared to have pipes built into his body. He sang praises to God. He was pretty much a minister in the Father's heavenly home.

Pastor Doug Batchelor, a Christian author and speaker, stated that the European cuckoo bird hen is notorious for laying her eggs in another bird's nest. She may even push one of the other bird's eggs out in the process. The cuckoo chick will usually hatch first, and then it will also push out any other eggs. The mother of the lost eggs then nurtures, feeds, and protects the cuckoo chick, thinking it's her own and not knowing the difference.[5] This is what the enemy does when he comes to a house of worship. He wants to plant his perverted theology and kick out the unadulterated Gospel that is water to our souls. Satan physically and spiritually pushes people out of a church, sometimes replacing them with others who are more aligned with his agenda. This is just one of his primary goals within godly places of worship.

Is Your Camp Holy?

According to the Scripture I quoted at the beginning of this chapter, your camp must be holy because God is in the midst of it to set you free and defeat your enemies. If He sees anything indecent among you, He will turn away.

Sin can be so abundant in a place (even a church) that the Lord will actually turn away from it. You can turn away from a person and still be in the same room. According to Deuteronomy 31:8, the Lord will never leave us nor forsake us. Yet I have been in churches where the *tangible* presence of God was not there.

I'm referring to ministries where you just don't feel Him in the building. I won't go as far as to say that the Lord isn't in those churches. The author of Psalm 139:8 wrote that if he makes his bed in hell, God is there. Remember, the Lord is omnipresent, according to Colossians 1:17. He is everywhere at once. However, God does not always make His presence known in a setting that dishonors Him by allowing another spirit to dominate that house.

God Warned Me . . .

Several years ago, my wife and I made plans to visit the church of a new friend. They were having a prophetic conference. Before we left for the event, the Lord began to speak to me. He said, *When you get there, the guest preacher is going to call you up and give you a prophetic word, but it's going to be off.*

In other words, it would be an inaccurate prophecy that didn't come from God. That should have been my cue not to go, but because I had a hard head and a stiff neck, we went anyway. Honestly, I really wanted to see if it would happen as the Lord said.

The visiting apostle began by prophesying to my wife, and surprisingly, he was very accurate. Then, as God had foretold, he asked me to come up. With a wide grin, he began to give his prophetic forecast for my life. He said that he saw water coming down from the sky and hitting a rock, but that it wasn't a good thing, because the water should be hitting the grass and causing growth, not hitting a rock. Then he added, "This year, you have been getting the results of an ant."

I was confused. The ant is one of the busiest insects of them all! Proverbs 6:6 admonishes us against laziness, using the ant as an example. I once totally decimated an ant hill in my backyard in the evening, and by the next morning they had completely rebuilt it.

This person's prediction didn't exemplify busyness, but a lack of divine opportunity and godly success that he presumptuously thought dominated my life. That year, however, had been one of the busiest and most productive of my entire ministerial career. The apostle noticed my bewilderment and then told me that I would be the recipient of two million dollars. Wow! I'm still waiting on that word to be fulfilled.

After he finished, the guest minister did the worst thing of all—he laid his hand on my head to pray for me. When we got home that evening, a demonic presence was on me (not in me), a presence I believe was transferred by that man through the laying on of his hands. It was oppressive, dark, and heavy. I prayed through the night, and it finally lifted. Praise God!

There are places you shouldn't go. Everything can't share space with you. I learned a couple of lessons from this encounter. First, I should have heeded the word of the Lord and stayed home when He told me what would transpire. Second, I should never have allowed the man to touch me. Third, I should have immediately and verbally rejected that false word of knowledge and walked away. Nothing is wrong with saying "I don't receive that" when hearing prophetic words that you know are wrong. Truth be told, I strongly suggest you do just that. I went into an environment that was unhealthy due to who and what was let in. (Please understand that this is not an indictment of the host at that church, whom I believe is authentic.)

Occasionally, we allow people in our environments whom we believe are godly, but they're not. I've made the same mistake more than once. They end up being representatives of the evil one while disguised as ministers of righteousness. The apostle Paul clearly identified these types of ministers:

> For such are false apostles, deceitful workers, transforming themselves into apostles of Christ. And no wonder! For Satan himself transforms himself into an angel of light. Therefore it is no great thing if his ministers also transform themselves into ministers of righteousness, whose end will be according to their works.
>
> 2 Corinthians 11:13–15

Unfortunately, quite a few of these ministers are working for the devil. When the Lord tells you not to go certain places, don't go. Your very life may depend on it. At times, the Lord has instructed me to stay home and I haven't listened—and I've paid a price for my disobedience each time. Hebrews 3:15 tells us, "Today, if you will hear His voice, do not harden your hearts as in the rebellion." Pay close attention to the voice of the Lord and obey Him.

Lay Hands on No One Suddenly

At this junction, I must warn you to be acutely careful of whom you permit to lay hands on you, even in church services or at other ministerial events. At times, I've allowed ministers like the one I just mentioned to do this to me, and I've suffered for it. They would put their hands on me, "*prophe-lie*" (give an untrue prophetic word), and impart something of suspect origin. I'd go home and end up having problems sleeping, feeling an evil presence nearby and an overall lack of peace.

Whenever someone lays hands on you, the distinct possibility exists of a spiritual transference or impartation. If the person is godly, it shouldn't be demonic. But if the person is bound by habitual or purposeful sin, that same sin may be imparted to you because you were unwittingly receptive to it. For example, if a minister is regularly committing adultery and he or she lays hands on you, that sin and the demon behind it may influence your actions in regard to sexual immorality. From now on, you shouldn't care how religiously incorrect it may appear not to allow someone to touch you. Just politely tell the person, "Please don't put your hands on me, my spouse, or my children." The person might get angry, but so be it. If he or she does react that way, then that individual probably wasn't hearing from the Lord in the first place.

Some speakers may not mean you any harm, but the demonic residue from their surroundings may get on you. For example, suppose a person's family was into voodoo. That individual escaped that environment, but the demonic residue remains. Then that person places his or her hands on you to pray. What's left of that residue can get on you. Now you're facing the consequences of someone else's warfare that you may or may not be prepared for.

First Timothy 5:22 (KJV) says, "Lay hands suddenly on no man, neither be partaker of other men's sins: keep thyself pure." The Greek word for *suddenly* here is *tachus*.[6] This verse's meaning is analogous to doing something quickly or hastily. Bible scholars say that this Scripture refers to prematurely sending novices into ministry. In my experience, it can also imply not putting your hands on people without asking. A person should never touch you without getting consent to do so first. Likewise, an individual should ask a husband before laying hands on his wife or children. If this isn't done, it's out of order and possibly not of God.

If you've allowed anyone to lay hands on you whom you were unsure about, pray against any demonic impartations, prayers, declarations, or assignments that came or might still come against you and your family as a result. If that doesn't work, deliverance may be in order.

Demonic Infiltration of a Church

The demonic infiltration of a church can happen through the people present and their actions. I visited a church years ago that I absolutely loved, but one encounter stands out that illustrated the hazards of being in the wrong place at the wrong time. The service was uplifting, and the personal ministry rich. The pastor began to pray and speak in the gift of other tongues.

All of a sudden, many of the congregants started doing the same. The odd thing was that some of them just were repeating his unknown tongues. He would say something like, "*Shaba doo domo*," and they would say verbatim, "*Shaba doo domo.*" It didn't agree with my spirit at all. What made it worse was that the guy sitting next to me was doing the same thing. My spirit was so grieved. I refused to participate and hurriedly headed for the exit.

When I got to my car, I felt a dark spirit crouched on the upper part of my back. I had never felt this before. When I got home to my wife, she greeted me, but I immediately told her not to speak to me because something inhumanly evil was on me. It felt like a *spirit of murder*. I rushed to our bedroom and slammed the door. I went into intense spiritual warfare against this thing, and within hours, the entity was totally gone. Straightaway, the Lord's peace overwhelmed me. Hallelujah!

I believe that this spirit of murder came from the guy who was sitting next to me in the service, reciting the pastor's tongues. Again, I felt grieved by the practice, and due to my proximity to this person, whatever was in him inadvertently got on me. The gift of tongues comes from the Father, not from other people. If one person simply mimics someone else's supernatural language, then God is not the author of it, because most tongues are different for each person. There is another, more sinister author who is a rank opportunist and who has an unspeakably ungodly agenda. When something doesn't agree with your spirit, don't have anything to do with it!

When I first began to operate in the gift of tongues, I sounded like a newborn baby (making simple sounds like *ga-ga, goo-goo*). I thought my unknown tongues were demonic and told my then-pastor so, looking for godly direction. He provided a great illustration. He asked me, "When babies are born, what do they sound like?"

I replied, "*Ga-ga, goo-goo.*"

"Exactly," he said. "It's only as babies grow older that their language develops. It's the same with speaking in tongues."

That made perfect sense to me. For me, it happened just as he said. As I matured in the spirit, so did my gift of tongues. My words in the Spirit became more advanced and intelligible. Acts 2:4 and Ephesians 6:18 let us know that this way of speaking is given to God's children as a gift and provides evidence of the indwelling of the Holy Spirit.

Accidentally Activating Demons

As the story I just shared with you about people repeating tongues shows, you can pick up demons even in a church service because they use individuals as vehicles. One example of this was when I was doing prophetic activations in a church out of state. Prophetic activations are simply exercises that strengthen and stir up the gift of prophecy within a believer. (For more information about this and also more on the prophetic, I highly recommend getting my book *Supernaturally Prophetic: A Practical Guide for Prophets and Prophetic People*.) Two of our ministry leaders, my wife and an elder, accompanied me on this trip as my assistants. I began the activation sessions the way I normally do. All seemed well until two of the people participating in the sessions began to manifest demonically. They were yelling, growling, and clenching their hands.

My wife and my elder jumped into action immediately! They ministered deliverance to both, resulting in freedom from those particular evil spirits that were disturbed by the activations.

When I returned home, I asked my covering apostle, a master in these types of activations, if people manifesting demons had ever happened to him while he was doing such activations. He replied, "No!"

I had a revelation after this foreign encounter. I decided that before I did any further activations, I would make sure that everyone participating knew Jesus Christ as his or her Lord and Savior. That's far more important than stirring up a gift. Now, I routinely ask participants if they're saved. In past sessions, I had always assumed that everyone involved was.

What this taught me is that just because people are in a godly setting doesn't mean that they can't bring demons in with them. We must be ever vigilant when it comes to the environments we find ourselves in, knowing that the enemy may be there as well.

The Third-Eye Incident

The devil infiltrates churches by posing as the Holy Spirit and speaking to ministers. A man or woman of God might enter a pulpit prepared to give the word of the Lord, but somehow, the enemy taints the message. We encountered this kind of ministry once a few years ago. On a windy evening in the city of Chicago, a guest minister came to preach at our church. This individual ministered a great message to our congregants, but made the mistake of advising them to do something demonic. Our guest urged them to open their "third eye" in reference to the prophetic and use this invisible eye to see more clearly into the spirit realm.

My jaw dropped! I had always known this minister to be an excellent teacher of the Word of God. At first, I looked at it as an unfortunate mistake, but I discerned the enemy's handiwork on further inspection. First, let's look at what a *third eye* is. According to Dictionary.com,

> The *third eye* is a representation of mystical intuition and insight—an inner vision and enlightenment beyond what the physical eyes can see. It is traditionally depicted as being located in the middle of the forehead.[7]

This definition goes on to say even more:

> One of the most powerful and important gods in Hinduism, Shiva, is often depicted with a *third eye*, representing his wisdom and enlightenment—but also representing the power of destruction. . . .
> *Third eye* is used by yogis and yoga practitioners, the New Age movement, and other spiritual practitioners to refer to the chakra and the spiritual vision it is believed to confer. . . .
> Be aware that the third eye has been used as a vulgar slang term for the *anus*.[8]

Now, does that sound godly to you? Me either. Our visiting minister probably meant no ill toward us as a body of believers. As I mentioned, people can be used by Satan unawares. They can speak on his behalf and be ignorant of it. Peter is a prime example of this. In Matthew 16, Jesus foretold His death and resurrection in the presence of His disciples, and through Peter, the devil had something to say:

> Then Peter took Him aside and began to rebuke Him, saying, "Far be it from You, Lord; this shall not happen to You!"
> But He turned and said to Peter, "Get behind Me, Satan! You are an offense to Me, for you are not mindful of the things of God, but the things of men."

> Matthew 16:22–23

The devil did not possess Peter in this case, but he did speak through him. This can be commonplace, even for a Christian. Satan can get his words out through us only if we listen to and repeat them. This is exactly what the apostle Peter did. Jesus didn't respond to Peter directly, but to the devil, who used Peter as a conduit for his iniquitous master plan. Satan still does this today, specifically targeting the Church. In Peter's situation, the apostle meant well. His love for Jesus prevented him from seeing Jesus' sacrificial mission from God. Peter let the enemy use him without realizing it. If we're not careful, the same thing can happen to us.

Some theologians say that the devil had no idea that Jesus' death, burial, and resurrection would result in his own eventual and eternal defeat. If this assertion is true, then why did he speak through Peter in an effort to prevent it from occurring? As a counterpoint to this theological position, Luke 22:3 says that "Then Satan entered Judas, surnamed Iscariot, who was numbered among the twelve," and Judas subsequently betrayed our Lord. If the devil knew that this act of treachery would lead to the cross and Jesus' death, burial, and resurrection, then why would he use Judas to do it?

As the author of confusion, sometimes the enemy does things that make no sense. His desire to destroy overrides his reason and logic. My main point here is for you to take note of how the enemy spoke through both our visiting preacher and the apostle Peter. Even though we're in a new era, the devil still utilizes the same old subterfuges. He will use any individuals who avail themselves to him. Honestly, in Judas's case, the door opened to the enemy because of sin, his fulfillment of biblical prophecy, and the state of his heart. The devil was already influencing him to steal money prior to fully possessing him (see John 12:6). This was a heart issue. Seeds of deceit were already planted there.

Lucifer can speak through anyone who listens to him with fidelity. The same thing happened with Job's wife when, in the midst of their calamity, she told her husband to curse God and die (see Job 2:9). Job's spouse said precisely what Satan had told God that Job would do in Job 1. So the enemy spoke to Job through her. That's what he still does today. At times, the enemy will speak not just through your adversaries, but through those who are closest to you (see Matthew 10:36). This is exactly what happens in church.

Witches and Warlocks in Disguise

Be aware, too, that witches and warlocks in disguise are joining churches. Under the guise of ministers or caring lay persons, they may cozy up to you during service, get your contact information, and gain your trust in order to try to sabotage your destiny in God. As I was studying for an upcoming episode of my podcast *Supernaturally Prophetic*, the Lord dropped this in my spirit: *Witches are infiltrating the Church disguised as prophets.*

This took me back to something that took place in our church. A woman whom I'll call Jill joined our ministry. She came in with a strong gift of prophecy that hadn't been properly cultivated. I felt as though we, as a prophetic ministry, could really help her. She appeared very humble, faithful, and sweet. One day, I gave her a word of knowledge that appeared to shake her up a bit. I told her that I saw witchcraft in her lineage and that we needed to break that spirit over her life through the ministry of deliverance. I articulated this carefully, respectfully, and encouragingly, but she didn't take it as such. A couple of days later, we spoke about it again, and she admitted that I was correct. All seemed well for a short time.

The next thing I knew, Jill had taken a couple of church members under her wing, mentoring and spiritually mothering them without my knowledge or approval. She eventually left our church, taking her spiritual children with her. I later confronted her, and she had an excuse for everything I brought to her.

The ministry Jill went to ordained her to a position that seemingly wasn't what she wanted, so she left there too. She then joined another church organization, and went on from there to start her own ministry. What I didn't mention is that I had confirmed her as a prophet because I felt as though God had called her to that gift (office). Did I miss the Lord? Quite possibly. I didn't see the witchcraft, manipulation, and her personal agenda until much later in her tenure at our church.

When agents of Satan join a church, sometimes they're difficult to identify. The enemy often uses membership within the body of a church as a favored avenue in his attempt to disable or kill the church. Like cancer, he gets in and metastasizes, attacking whatever organ (person) he gets close to. This is why it's so important to ask the Lord repeatedly to increase your level of discernment.

Demonic Infiltration through Leadership

The enemy can infiltrate the Church in multiple ways. One of his preferred methods is through leadership. If he can get the head, then the body will follow. The head is the leader of the body; as the head goes, so the body will go. This is why many pastors go through so much hell. The devil uses demonic tactics to discredit, disgrace, and destroy the reputation (name) of the leader in order to discourage or disperse the congregation.

There are times when a leader of a church allows Satan to get in, and the congregants suffer. He or she does this by engaging in persistent sin. The world, unfortunately, has seen this happen far too often. It remains a blemish on the Church as a whole. That's why we must be both cautious and observant when it comes to the enemy: "Be sober, be vigilant; because your adversary the devil walks about like a roaring lion, seeking whom he may devour" (1 Peter 5:8).

I recently heard a cautionary tale about a pastor who was an extremely gifted orator. He had a large, thriving church, and many doors of opportunity had opened for him. Before many of his speaking engagements, he would use illegal drugs, and he would have sex with various women afterward. The powers that be found out about his unholy extracurricular activities, and he ended up losing his position as senior leader. Sadly, not long after, this minister tragically lost his life at a young age.

Scripture lets us know that the consequence (wages) of sin is death (see Romans 6:23). The enemy is banking on this when he places temptation in front of us. The Bible also alerts us to the fact that the devil's time is short and that he's filled with fury (see Revelation 12:12). With his limited time in mind, Satan wants to kill the reputation (name) of as many of the saints as he can. The following Scripture admonishes us to consider carefully becoming a teacher in the house of the Lord: "My brethren, let not many of you become teachers, knowing that we shall receive a stricter judgment" (James 3:1).

Anything Goes These Days

In this current era, it seems as if anything goes, and the devil loves it. If church leadership as a whole is not living holy, in time unholiness will infect the entire Ecclesia (Church). According to Hebrews 12:14, we must "work at living in peace with everyone, and work at living a holy life, for those who are not holy will not see the Lord" (NLT).

I personally have seen bars for serving alcohol set up at church gatherings. I have witnessed church members "twerking" to secular music at ministry celebrations. To clarify, the *Merriam-Webster Dictionary* defines *twerking* as "sexually suggestive dancing characterized by rapid, repeated hip thrusts and shaking of the buttocks especially while squatting."[9] Does this sound like anything that should be seen in the Church? I don't think so either.

I've heard pastors use profanity in the pulpit. I knew a leader who would get involved in adulterous sexual relationships right after preaching Sunday services. Some of the aforementioned incidents were perpetrated, committed, or sanctioned by church leadership. In these examples, the leaders created hazardous environments. Many individuals, including Christians, have lost *the fear of the Lord* in this era. I'm not talking about a cowardly type of fear, but the reverential kind:

> The [reverent] fear of the LORD [that is, worshiping Him and regarding Him as truly awesome] is the beginning and the pre-eminent part of wisdom [its starting point and its essence], And the knowledge of the Holy One is understanding and spiritual insight.
>
> Proverbs 9:10 AMP

Lord, Are You Sure?

Years ago, I asked the Lord to show me the church that I was supposed to join. As a relatively new Christian at the time, I needed a solid ecclesiastical home. I narrowed it down to two. I prayed concerning them both, and God selected one for me. The next Sunday, I found myself in a church that was not to my particular liking, but as I sat down in one of the pews, I heard the Lord say, *This is where I would have you, but only for a season.* After a couple of weeks of visiting, I became a member of this church. The pastor and his wife were very welcoming and friendly.

Please forgive me for this next part, but I want to be totally transparent. The place was terrible, and it had a very foul odor to it! It wasn't good at all, from the preaching to the people to the leadership. I was like, *Lord, are you sure you want me here?*

To my dismay, He was sure. Elisa started coming with me, but refused to join the church. She stated that God hadn't told her to. I was without delay ordained as a deacon, but without my consent or approval. (They had few members and were eager to fill leadership positions.) The pastor just told me one day that

I would be their deacon and abruptly gave me an ordination certificate. I seemingly had no say in the matter.

About a year later, the pastor called me into his office. He stated that it was my job as the deacon to pay all the church's bills. *What?* My wife and I lived in an attic apartment and didn't have much money at the time. We were saving for our first home. I politely declined. The pastor was adamant that the Lord would find a way for us to do it. I left the office confused. He must have thought we were awfully gullible. But please don't mistake our zeal for the things of the Lord for stupidity. After prayerful consideration, I informed him that we would not be taking on that financial responsibility.

My much-older pastor routinely flirted with my wife. I found out much later that he had previously cheated on his spouse. As time passed, I felt a check in my spirit that my time there was coming to an end. I met with him to let him know we would be leaving. I added that God had told me I would only be there for a season. This leader replied that a season was a period of time that could mean a lifetime.

I left that pastor's office with the mindset of seeking confirmation from the Lord. One night, I had a dream that gave me just that. In it, I saw myself walking into that church, looking for my wife. She and the pastor were coming out of the back room. I noticed that his hair was disheveled and his clothing was rumpled. Before I could inquire as to what was going on, there was a great rumbling in the building. To my horror, the ceiling began to collapse. I woke up knowing that the Lord had spoken. The very next day, I left that ministry and never looked back.

About six months later, I received word that the roof of the church had actually collapsed in real life! From day one, this was a hazardous environment, but it was also a learning experience. I discovered so much about what *not* to do in ministry. It helped me a lot later on in my ministerial life. At times, you will be called by God to certain places and not totally understand why. While you are in such a place, the enemy will do his best to get you to leave before your time. In my case, the Father was directing me, and I stayed until He led me out.

We talked a few times in these pages about how in Matthew 4, the Spirit led Jesus into the wilderness to be tempted by the devil. This was a hazardous situation mainly because Satan was there, but it was *pregnant with a purpose*. After Jesus passed the test, He walked in greater power and authority. Wherever you are, endure the warfare until the Lord tells you otherwise. Like Jesus, you will come out of that place with added weight and influence in the Spirit, if you were led there by Him.

YOUR BATTLE PLAN

Ask God to increase your level of discernment. Pray about every environment where you may feel led to go. Seek the Lord regarding who, what, and where to submit yourself. Listen attentively to the Lord when He speaks to you concerning certain places. You can do this during your regular times of prayer by listening more than you speak. For example, if you pray for one hour, spend at least thirty minutes listening to God's response. No matter what surroundings you find yourself in, put on the full armor of God and never take it off! I strongly urge you to read the Scripture that follows daily, especially before entering locations you're getting a check in your spirit about. If you can memorize it, that would be ideal:

> Put on all of God's armor so that you will be able to stand firm against all strategies of the devil. For we are not fighting against flesh-and-blood enemies, but against evil rulers and authorities of the unseen world, against mighty powers in this dark world, and against evil spirits in the heavenly places.

Therefore, put on every piece of God's armor so you will be able to resist the enemy in the time of evil. Then after the battle you will still be standing firm. Stand your ground, putting on the belt of truth and the body armor of God's righteousness. For shoes, put on the peace that comes from the Good News so that you will be fully prepared. In addition to all of these, hold up the shield of faith to stop the fiery arrows of the devil.

Ephesians 6:11–16 NLT

YOUR BATTLE PRAYER

Father God, in the name of Jesus, I ask you to protect me from all hazardous environments. If I ever find myself in one, I pray that it will be on purpose, for a purpose, and orchestrated by you. I will come out of it in due season stronger than I was when I went in. Please show me the correct spiritual table I should be eating from and its location, and I will go. Lord, sharpen my ability to discern what's of you and what's not of you.

I bind every demon that attempts to usurp my destiny by urging me to engage in and utilize demonic dialogue. I come against the devil speaking through me. Lord, allow me to perceive false teachings, avoid demonic leadership, and identify the carriers of your glory. If I encounter any witch or warlock, I will have no fear. In fact, I will do my best to redirect the person to you so he or she can benefit from your saving grace.

I come against an "anything goes" spirit. It will have no place in me. Lord, I will listen to you when you tell me not to go somewhere. I will not let anyone lay hands on me unless I know the person is of you. If the devil ever joins my church, I have the power, ability, and authority to cancel his membership. According to Ephesians 6, I will keep your full armor on, Lord, and never take it off. I will even sleep in it. Lord, I thank you that demonic lions cannot devour me because I am protected by the Lion of the Tribe of Judah. Father, I thank you for giving me eyes to see and ears to hear what the Spirit of the Lord is saying and showing me concerning every major step that I take. Hallelujah!

(Note: Praise God now to seal the effectiveness of this battle prayer.)

You Will Prevail!

Announcing the Rise of the Jacob Generation

And He said, "Your name shall no longer be called Jacob, but Israel; for you have struggled with God and with men, and have prevailed."

—Genesis 32:28

A couple of years ago, I was conversing with a friend about the next generation of church leaders. We both had our reservations about them. I referred to how different they are from the previous generation in so many ways, from how they dress to how they worship, to their tattoos. The Lord showed me a generation of believers who looked nothing like the ones in times past. They would start off as rebellious, sinful, arrogant, deceptive, judgmental know-it-alls. My colleague referred to them as *the Jacob generation*.

This summarized what I had been seeing in the spirit for years. At first I was troubled by it, but I knew the Lord was going to use the generation I was seeing to start the type of revivals that hadn't been seen in decades. My friend and I proceeded to discuss how in Scripture, because of his deceptive ways, Jacob was on the run from the Lord and his brother, Esau (see Genesis 27). Yet he would soon have a supernatural encounter with Jehovah. This meeting would change not only his name but also his nature.

This stimulating discourse led me to study Jacob a bit further. Jacob, whose name in Hebrew is יַעֲקֹב (*Ya'aqov*), was the son of Isaac and Rebecca. His name means "usurper or supplanter," a person who seizes, circumvents, or usurps. It also means "one who follows behind" and "the holder of the heel."[1] That is basically what Jacob did most of his life. Genesis 3:15 speaks of the serpent's offspring bruising the heel of the woman's seed. Satan wanted Jacob to bruise Esau's heel, but instead, he held it as they were being born. This is representative of the spirit of competition that I alluded to in chapter 5. Jacob dealt with various struggles throughout his entire life, but everything changed when he struggled with God and won. "In the womb he grasped his brother's heel; as a man he struggled with God. He struggled with the angel and overcame him; he wept and begged for his favor" (Hosea 12:3–4 NIV).

Genesis 27:36 (NLT) indicates that Esau was not surprised that his brother's name was Jacob: "Esau exclaimed, 'No wonder his name is Jacob, for now he has cheated me twice. First, he took my rights as the firstborn, and now he has stolen my blessing. Oh, haven't you saved even one blessing for me?'" Esau lamented that his younger brother stole not only his birthright but also his blessing. This was not unusual behavior for Jacob. Each time Jacob's name was spoken, the definition of it manifested even more in his life.

In another example, the name Yosemite means "those who kill" or "killers."[2] Every time you say that person's name to him or her, you're essentially calling the person a killer. Now, I'm not saying every person will act out the meaning of his or her name. However, I am saying that when you continually speak something into someone's life, the person can possibly come to exemplify and walk out what you speak. Jacob *became* his name.

What's your name? What does it mean? My name is John. It comes from the Hebrew *Yohanan*, which means favored by God, and also that the Lord has been merciful. Has the Lord been merciful to me? Yes, on many occasions. Praise His holy name! Have I been graced or favored by the Lord? Without a doubt. Did I deserve it? Not at all. I truly believe that my name has had something to do with that.

But I'm getting a little ahead of myself. Jacob was a trickster, and throughout his life, his antics were on display in almost everything he did. When we act deceptively, it will eventually catch up to us. Galatians 6:7 instructs us that we will reap what we sow. Jacob definitely was a recipient of the deception he had been sowing for years. In one instance, he was misled by his mother's brother Laban regarding Rachel and Leah, his uncle's daughters. Jacob was promised the beautiful Rachel as his wife, but was deceived into first marrying her older, less attractive sister, Leah (see Genesis 29). There was also another instance when Jacob feared his imminent reunion with Esau, and he sort of came to the end of himself (see Genesis 33). His growth into maturity, his life experiences, and the warm welcome he got from Esau— even after deceiving his brother into giving up his birthright—all contributed to Jacob's change of nature.

New Name, New Nature

To cement his transmutation, Jacob needed a new name. The Lord knew that he was in a preordained position to receive it:

> During the night, Jacob got up and took his two wives, his two servant wives, and his eleven sons and crossed the Jabbok River with them. After taking them to the other side, he sent over all his possessions.

This left Jacob all alone in the camp, and a man came and wrestled with him until the dawn began to break. When the man saw that he would not win the match, he touched Jacob's hip and wrenched it out of its socket. Then the man said, "Let me go, for the dawn is breaking!"

But Jacob said, "I will not let you go unless you bless me."

"What is your name?" the man asked.

He replied, "Jacob."

"Your name will no longer be Jacob," the man told him. "From now on you will be called Israel, because you have fought with God and with men and have won."

"Please tell me your name," Jacob said.

"Why do you want to know my name?" the man replied. Then he blessed Jacob there.

Jacob named the place Peniel (which means "face of God"), for he said, "I have seen God face to face, yet my life has been spared." The sun was rising as Jacob left Peniel, and he was limping because of the injury to his hip. (Even today the people of Israel don't eat the tendon near the hip socket because of what happened that night when the man strained the tendon of Jacob's hip.)

Genesis 32:22–32 NLT

The crossing of the Jabbok River was definitely a prophetic act for Jacob. He did this because he needed God to bless him. He realized that the most opportune time to hear the voice of God is when you're alone, with little to no distractions. This instinctual action symbolized the birthing of an evacuation from Jacob's previous position, nature, and stature. It was the genesis of the dissipation or disappearance of his current name. He was about to have a wrestling match with the preincarnate Christ that would shift his life's quality, direction, and intentionality.

Notice in Genesis 32:24 that the "man" (the preincarnate Christ) initiated the match with Jacob. He could have ended it at any time, but He didn't until He saw a change in Jacob. A purpose was attached to this particular conflict. It was part of Jacob's destiny and necessary for his progression, future blessings, and makeover into the man God had called him to be. This metamorphosis could not happen for "Jacob," but it could for "Israel." And it's the same for us.

What's in a Name? Everything!

Lots of times, we have to struggle through the process when we're called by the Lord. If you can survive the process, then the authorization will be provided. Once He authorizes you, the Lord commissions you for the call He has placed upon your life. With this comes a name change, and with the name change comes a new assignment. In Jacob's situation, he was determined not to allow the "man" to leave until He blessed him. This man asked Jacob his name in Genesis 32:27, and he replied, "Jacob." This time he told the truth, but this had not been the case only a couple of chapters earlier. In Genesis 27:18–19, when Isaac asked the son bringing him food his name, Jacob had lied, saying, "I am Esau." Honesty with God about your identity will move His hand on your behalf to bless you.

Regarding Jacob's confession of his real name to the Lord, and His possible response, Pastor Bruce Goettsche wrote this paraphrase:

> "You have spoken the truth," God said, "and you know very well what your name signifies. You have been a duplicitous man, deceiving everyone everywhere you went. But now that you acknowledge the real you, I can change you, and I will make a great nation out of you."[3]

Pastor Goettsche commented further, "So, why did the angel ask for his name? He asked for his name not because he didn't know it . . . he wanted to know if Jacob knew his name!"[4]

God will ask your name not because He doesn't know it, but just to see if you do. Jacob needed to reach the point where he had no more strength left. He wanted God's blessing, but didn't want God's ownership of his life. In his wrestling, he was left with an injury that caused him to walk with a limp for the rest of his life. This was his badge of honor. Pastor Goettsche also wrote that scars have a tendency to remind us of what we've learned.[5] The scars of life tend to remind us of all the warfare we've been through.

In the spirit, I see people involved in various types and states of sin being transformed when they come to the end of themselves. This is what took place with Jacob. At times in our lives, lasting change can only happen when we hit rock bottom. These individuals I'm seeing may have participated in sins such as drunkenness, excessive and long-term partying, using illegal drugs, fornicating, involvement in homosexuality, prostitution, etc., but just like the prodigal son mentioned in Luke 15:11–32, there will be a homecoming. Verse 17 says that the prodigal son "came to himself." The Jacobs of the next generation are at the end of themselves and are presently coming to themselves—their *true selves*—in the Lord. They are slowly but surely morphing into "Israels," ones who have wrestled with the preincarnate Christ, striven with Him, and won with Him.

These individuals will be fighters for God instead of fighting against Him. There is a difference. Please don't make the mistake of fighting the Lord instead of wrestling with Him. Wrestling is a more intimate type of conflict, while a battle is usually fought against an enemy. You don't fight God; you wrestle with Him. That's the only way you will prevail.

In Acts 5, Jesus' disciples were preaching the Gospel, and the members of the Sanhedrin wanted to kill them. As the *Merriam-Webster Dictionary* tells us, the Sanhedrin was "the supreme council and tribunal of the Jews during postexilic times headed by a High Priest and having religious, civil, and criminal jurisdiction."[6] But one member, a Pharisee named Gamaliel, an expert in religious law who was respected by all the people, defended the disciples. He cited Theudas and Judas (not Iscariot), whose campaigns had amounted to nothing because the Lord wasn't the originator of them. Gamaliel emphasized to the other council members that if what the disciples were doing was not of God, it wouldn't prosper. "But if it is from God," he said, "you will not be able to overthrow them. You may even find yourselves fighting against God!" (Acts 5:39 NLT).

The Twenty-Year Wait

I've been seeing variations of the number 20 for most of my life. In fact, I still see it today, sometimes on a license plate, on a building, or even in a room number. I was born on February 20th (2/20). A minister in college once told me that 220 would be the number on the door of the room I would die in. That hasn't happened yet, thank God! This number always seemed to have a negative connotation for my future. The year 2020, two twenties, brought the worldwide pandemic of the deadly COVID-19 virus (which I wrote about extensively in chapter 2).

Twenty is one more than nineteen and twice the amount of ten, and can sometimes mean a complete or perfect waiting period. For a total of twenty years, Jacob waited to be freed from the control of Laban, his father-in-law (see Genesis 31:38–41). After working for Laban for seven years, Jacob's initial reward was Laban's daughter Leah in marriage, whom he didn't want. Then after seven more years he finally got Rachel, whom he had wanted all along. For the first seven years, he worked for something he didn't get because of Laban's deception in giving him Leah. He toiled an additional seven years to get the wife he had first wanted, Rachel. Then he worked six more years for his flocks. By enduring the "perfect waiting period," 20 years working for Laban, Jacob received what he truly wanted.

As I write these pages, I am hearing this word in my spirit: *The Jacobs of today will also be deceived initially into living in a way that the Lord did not intend. Later, they will receive the proper commission from God and will run with it. The spirit of Laban will no longer restrain them. Their wait will number twenty years. They will cry loud and spare not, offending only the most religious and the unsaved. The sound that proceeds out of them will be like a trumpet. They will call out sin and confess their own sins without reservation or shame. Transparency will be their hallmark, so that many believe that they carry the Word, the oil, and the heart of the Most High. "Cry aloud, spare not; lift up your voice like a trumpet; tell My people their transgression, and the house of Jacob their sins" (Isaiah 58:1).*

I sense that beginning in 2000, the complete or perfect waiting period began for the emergence of this group of usurpers, liars, and supplanters—in other words, these Jacobs. They found themselves muddled in the consequences of their sinful activities. In 2020, a transformation occurred. They repented and desired a change in their natures. They knew by the Spirit of the Lord that it was their time of conversion. At first, they fought the Lord, His people, His Word, and His Church. Yes, these Jacobs started off fighting God; now they're beginning to wrestle with Him.

The Lord will give this whole group or generation new names in the spirit during this wrestling match. The Jacobs of this arising generation (tricksters/deceivers) will contend for righteousness during this time. Great revival will mark their meetings. Many of them (and others) will get saved, delivered, and set free because they're done fighting against the Lord.

The Jacobs of this arising generation are now wrestling with God's Spirit, and He is allowing them to win. Remember, wrestling is an intimate form of combat. The more intimate we are with the Father, the more He transforms us. We wrestle with Him through prayer, fasting, deep study, worship, holiness, surrendering all, selling out, loving others, and obeying His commands.

When "Jacobs" wrestle, "Israels" win! The Jacobs only become Israels after an authentic encounter with the Father that changes their names and natures. Hallelujah!

Rachels, Arise!

The Jacob generation is not gender specific. Women will be at the forefront of this move of God because they were the first to wrestle (more on that in a moment), and also, they are betrothed to the Jacobs. Once married, they will birth the next generation of world changers.

It's crucial to realize that Rachel didn't wrestle with the pre-incarnate Christ, but she did wrestle with the spirits of envy, self-doubt, and resentment. Apart from giving birth herself, she produced offspring for her husband through another vessel, her maid, Bilhah. Because of the influence of the Rachels, other women can give birth in the spirit. This will result in a multiplication of *princess warriors* who will come against the enemy, alongside the Israels. Jacob's wife wrestled and prevailed. Rachels, arise!

Now when Rachel saw that she bore Jacob no children, Rachel envied her sister, and said to Jacob, "Give me children, or else I die!"

And Jacob's anger was aroused against Rachel, and he said, "Am I in the place of God, who has withheld from you the fruit of the womb?"

So she said, "Here is my maid Bilhah; go in to her, and she will bear a child on my knees, that I also may have children by her." Then she gave him Bilhah her maid as wife, and Jacob went in to her. And Bilhah conceived and bore Jacob a son. Then Rachel said, "God has judged my case; and He has also heard my voice and given me a son." Therefore she called his name Dan. And Rachel's maid Bilhah conceived again and bore Jacob a second son. Then Rachel said, "With great wrestlings I have wrestled with my sister, and indeed I have prevailed." So she called his name Naphtali.

Genesis 30:1–8

Rachel had been wrestling for years before Jacob's wrestling match with God. Her conflict started with envy, but she indirectly conceived (through her handmaid Bilhah) when she wrestled with her sister. She wasn't really contending with her barrenness, but with jealousy. She was envious of those who could do what she could not. Though it looked as if she was struggling with her emotions, she was actually wrestling with principalities and powers birthed in dark places. These demons knew her seed would be anointed, so they didn't want Rachel and Jacob's children ever to see the light of day.

> For we are not wrestling with flesh and blood [contending only with physical opponents], but against the despotisms, against the powers, against [the master spirits who are] the world rulers of this present darkness, against the spirit forces of wickedness in the heavenly (supernatural) sphere.
>
> Ephesians 6:12 AMPC

When the Lord wrestled with Jacob, he wasn't named Israel yet. God was wrestling with a cheater, a liar, and a thief, based on the origin of Jacob's moniker. The outcome of their match turned him into Israel. The initial contest was between the Lord and the principalities behind Jacob's past deceitful actions. Wrestling was a type of deliverance for Jacob. When casting out demons, deliverance ministers usually wrestle with the demonic forces for some time before they achieve freedom for the individual. After his encounter with God, Jacob was delivered from himself.

While struggling with the enemy, don't fool yourself into thinking that you're contending with a physical foe. Too often, we spend an exorbitant amount of time striving with people, and we miss out on the fact that our battle is with principalities, powers, and wicked rulers in high places. Too many apostles, prophets, pastors, evangelists, and teachers are more at odds with each other than they are with Satan. Our warfare should be corporate, against a familiar foe. You're not alone in this battle. Don't be an island unto yourself. No man is an island unless God is on the island with him.

A Pivot in Our Focus

While we must discern our common enemy, at times our prevailing will require a shift or pivot in our focus. As I looked at several definitions of the word *pivot*, I combined them to create my own definition. This word means to turn, or to change position, policy, or strategy. It's an indication that there has been a shift or change in your stance, perspective, or direction. Instead of focusing on battling Satan, we must focus on wrestling with God. We should be making strenuous efforts to promote what the Kingdom dictates instead of the foolishness of the devil. This is precisely what the Jacob generation will do.

When you wrestle with God, *you win by losing*. Take into account, the "man" could have defeated Jacob at any given time. There was a purpose in that wrestling match. He wanted Jacob to see who he really was. This discovery brought about the blessing that Jacob desperately wanted. Again, he couldn't be legitimately blessed as Jacob, but he could be blessed as Israel.

Whenever you have an intense encounter with God, your name (nature) will be changed. Historically, some people in the Bible received a name change after a supernatural appointment with the Father:

1. Saul became Paul (see Acts 13:9).
2. Abram became Abraham (see Genesis 17:5).

3. Simon became Peter (see John 1:42 NLT).

4. Jacob became Israel (see Genesis 32:28).

Wrestling with God turns on an identity switch, followed by the blessing of elevation in Him. You may have to wrestle all night until you receive the blessings, but don't let go until He blesses you. Now, that's the type of faith that will move the heart and hand of the Lord! Once you touch God's heart, His hand will move—it has to. If you are not already doing this, you need to shift. Satan can do nothing that God does not allow (e.g., Job). So whatever trial you're going through at this moment that requires arduous effort, God allowed it. Don't fight it; wrestle with it. You will strive, and you will prevail!

The Jacob Generation's Rise

The former usurpers, liars, and supplanters who are rising up in this hour will struggle with God, man, and against the gods of this age in these dark and evil times 2 Timothy 3 speaks of. They may not look like what the Church had in mind. They may not sound like the Church thought they would sound. They might not look like what a Christian is *supposed* to look like. What proceeds out of them will be different from others who came before them. They are a new breed who will wrestle until they prevail and receive blessings from the Lord—not just for themselves, but for an entire generation. Although they may seem undesirable, seemingly lost in the eyes of others, they will receive new names and eventually transform into a cavalry of Israels—people who contend with God and man and win!

In fact, *the devil will need to get delivered from them*, because just as the preincarnate Christ did with Jacob in Scripture, these Jacobs will initiate battle with the evil one and not just wait for him to attack. They will refuse to "tithe to the devil." Many people do this ignorantly by giving at least 10 percent of their increase to Satanic endeavors (e.g., worldly concerts, demonic occupations, occult practices, dark entertainment, etc.). The ever-evolving Jacobs will lose interest in the realms of darkness. They will slowly but surely replace these demonically orchestrated vices with godly undertakings.

Some who are reading this right now are part of the Jacob generation. You are called to win the war against the enemy. While hell is breaking out all around you, you will be able to stand firm. You will be the remnant the apostle Paul prophesied about: "Even so then, at this present time there is a remnant" (Romans 11:5). I am expectant and elated about the remnant. If you are among them, you will help usher in weighty moves of the Spirit never seen before. As you develop into Israels, you will not tolerate the messiness that we witness in some churches today. Like David in Scripture, you will confront the Goliaths of your day (the dark rulers in high places) and win. Like David, you will kill those giants with their own weaponry.

A number of prophets will be in this group. They will declare the word of the Lord with no reservation, cowardice, or fear. They will speak the truth to power, not alarmed by the repercussions or damage to their names. Jacobs who are evolving into Israels will find themselves on the floors of legislative government, where they will be called to enact God's laws over Satan's. During this time, demons will start to flee from government institutions in record numbers. Their assaults on the Jacobs will intensify so that a number will quit before becoming Israels. But the remnant will remain, and a banner will be raised that will be carried by their sons and daughters for many generations to come.

Isolate yourself if you are one of these Jacobs. Use this time to hear the voice of the Lord. Wrestle with Him until He blesses you, so that you can bless others and prevail. Jacobs, arise and become the Israels of your day!

YOUR BATTLE PLAN

If you feel called as part of *the Jacob generation*, you must abide in the Lord as never before. Tune out every distraction that would exclude you from the remnant that the Lord is calling up and out in this season. Avoid sins such as fornication, lying, perversion, bearing false witness against your neighbor, gossiping, etc. Don't allow yourself to get tainted by ungodly music. Listen to anointed Christian music. Be careful where you go. The Lord will instruct you not to set your foot in some environments. As the Lord prospers you, never forget Him. Obey His commandments, regulations, and decrees (see Deuteronomy 8:11). Pray in tongues (in the Holy Spirit) every chance you get (see Jude 1:20). This will fortify and strengthen your spirit. Stand up against evil powers, and declare the word of the Lord.

YOUR BATTLE PRAYER

Father, in the name of your Son, Jesus Christ, I believe that I am part of the Jacob generation. I may not look like what has come before me, but I am called and chosen to be an agent of change for the world. I thank you that you have destined me for this specific time, to come against the forces of darkness, leading your children out of darkness and into the light. Lord, empower me to overcome every obstacle the enemy puts in my way. As your Word tells me in Isaiah 54:17, no weapon formed against me will work!

I join together with my brothers and sisters around the world in agreement that we will not be bound by Satan's status quo. The Jacob generation is not gender specific, either. I know Rachels are arising in every part of the globe. God, allow us all to connect and usher in a worldwide revival that will shake the planet. Souls will be won, addictions will be destroyed, witches and warlocks will repent, mental illness will be cured, the lame will be healed, and the spirit of suicide will be defeated. According to your Word in Luke 1:37, nothing is impossible for you!

I am an important part of the army of God, and I already have the victory. I am just awaiting the manifestation of it. Lord, endue me with your oil so I can be effective as a warrior for you. Amen.

(Note: One final time, seal this closing prayer with praise and worship.)

CONCLUSION

Jacobs and Rachels, Arise!

The people who know their God shall be strong, and carry
out great exploits.

—Daniel 11:32

There you have it—eight strategies that you can use to defeat
Satan's latest schemes. I listed these back in the introduction,
and then we looked at each one more closely in the chapters that
followed, but I want to list them for you here one final time. They
are (1) cutting soul ties, (2) avoiding occult activities, (3) fasting
and prayer, (4) guarding your mind, (5) protecting your hearing,
(6) being careful of your environment, (7) cleaning house, and
(8) abiding in Christ. (That eighth one means reading the Word,
praying without ceasing and in the Spirit, worshiping Jesus, and
assembling with other believers.)

I pray that you revisit this book often to review these strategies,
and to utilize the plans and prayers I've included within. As I've
mentioned, the enemy has harassed me throughout the entire

process of writing it, because he didn't want you to reach this point (the end of the book). Thankfully, you made it!

Although this is the conclusion, unfortunately it is not the end of the enemy's assaults on you and your family. Whenever you endeavor to do a work for the Lord, the devil will come against you. If he can't get to you directly, he will attack your loved ones. I truly believe that you are called to stand in the gap for your family. I view you as a potential warrior prince or princess within the regiment of the Most High God. Many people are voluntarily or involuntarily held hostage by Satan: witches, warlocks, and those who are in bondage to him through generational curses or who are marked by demons. As I touched on in the beginning, use what you've read in this book on the evil one so that *he will need deliverance from you.* It's time to take the offensive regarding bankrupting hell and populating the Kingdom of heaven with many of these lost souls.

Every day, even now, a brand-new level of evil is changing into a more heinous manifestation. I know that you can see and sense it threatening to snuff out the last bits of hope your heart clings to. But God always provides a way of escape, teaches your hands to war, and gives unlimited grace and wisdom. He is the consuming fire that sees what you're currently going through. He has battle plans and prayers that will ensure your overall peace, total freedom, and lasting victory. If you know of anyone struggling against demonic forces, then tell them about what you've learned. Along with a Bible, get them a copy of this book. I believe this will release the same freedom to them that, hopefully, you are experiencing.

Remember, the enemy has developed new schemes for today, but he really doesn't have any new tricks. He's just applying what he has used for ages, but in new avenues such as social media, AI technology, and the like. As Satan comes up with even more plans for these bold, modern times, I pray that you will be equipped by what the Lord has shown me, which I have shared with you.

Satan is already defeated in your life through the work of Jesus Christ on the cross. Keep in mind that you have the victory. You just have to walk in it. Glory to God!

Jacobs, arise! Rachels, arise! It's time for the greatest revival this world has ever seen. (I realize I've mentioned this several times, but it's just that important!) You are the reason the devil is fighting so hard. He knows his time is short. God's forces are growing each and every day, and you are part of the Lord's army. As we just read in Daniel 11:32, those who know their God will be strong and do exploits. As a Jacob or Rachel, you will wrestle and prevail. May the Lord continue to bless every divine endeavor that you embark upon. I pray that you will destroy every demonic tactic you face in life!

NOTES

Chapter 1 Identity and the Danger of "If Thous"

1. Vocabulary.com, s.v. "be," accessed November 22, 2023, https://www.vocabulary.com/dictionary/be.

2. Tiffany Robbins, "5 Key Ways to Study the Bible Like Charles Stanley," Crosswalk, April 20, 2023, https://www.crosswalk.com/special-coverage/charles-stanley-1932-2023/key-ways-to-study-the-bible-like-charles-stanley.html.

3. *Britannica Dictionary*, s.v. "identity," accessed November 22, 2023, https://www.britannica.com/dictionary/identity.

4. Alicia Britt Chole, *Anonymous: Jesus' Hidden Years . . . and Yours* (Nashville: Thomas Nelson, 2011), 115–116.

5. If you feel as though you need to hear God more clearly, I strongly urge you to take my class. It's called "Hearing Navigation: Tuning the Skill of Your Ear to the Voice of God," and it's on-demand, so it's available whenever you are. You can sign up by visiting https://www.johnvealschool.org/courses/hearingnavigation.

Chapter 2 The Current Pandemic

1. Mayo Clinic Staff, "Depression (major depressive disorder)," Mayo Clinic, October 14, 2022, https://www.mayoclinic.org/diseases-conditions/depression/symptoms-causes/syc-20356007.

2. "Youth Suicide Rates Increased During the COVID-19 Pandemic," National Institute of Mental Health, May 22, 2023, https://www.nimh.nih.gov/news/science-news/2023/youth-suicide-rates-increased-during-the-covid-19-pandemic.

3. For more information and a number of helpful articles on dealing with the various aspects of suicide as a Christian, visit Got Questions Ministries at https://www.gotquestions.org and do a search for "suicide."

4. For more on all of this, see "What Does the Bible Say about Suicide?," GotQuestions.org, accessed November 22, 2023, https://www.gotquestions.org /suicide-Bible-Christian.html.

5. "988 Frequently Asked Questions," Substance Abuse and Mental Health Services Administration, last updated June 15, 2023, https://www.samhsa.gov /find-help/988/faqs#.

6. *Oxford Learner's Dictionaries*, s.v. "therapist (*n.*)," accessed November 22, 2023, https://www.oxfordlearnersdictionaries.com/us/definition/american _english/therapist#.

7. Jeff Martin, "9 Tangible Benefits of Bible Reading for Your Church," Lifeway Research, January 20, 2021, https://research.lifeway.com/2021/01/20 /9-tangible-benefits-of-bible-reading-for-your-church.

8. Jacqueline Ramos, "Does God Care about My Mental Health?," The Center for Integrative Counseling and Psychology, May 18, 2021, https://thecenter counseling.org/articles/does-god-care-about-my-mental-health.

Chapter 3 The Battlefield Is Your Mind

1. James Chen, "Squatter: Definition, Example, Legal Rights," Investopedia, December 29, 2021, https://www.investopedia.com/terms/s/squatter.asp.

2. "Becoming the Owner of the Property by Using It for a Long Time," Illinois Legal Aid, May 24, 2020, https://www.illinoislegalaid.org/legal-information /becoming-owner-property-using-it-long-time.

Chapter 4 Spiritual Suicide

1. Jeremy Meyers, "God Sometimes Withdraws Protection," Redeeming God, accessed November 22, 2023, https://redeeminggod.com/god-sometimes -withdraws-protection.

2. The definitions and accompanying Scriptures in this paragraph are drawn from the material found in *Baker's Evangelical Dictionary*, s.v. "spirit (*n.*)," accessed November 22, 2023, https://www.biblestudytools.com/dictionaries/bakers -evangelical-dictionary/spirit.html.

3. John Eadie, quoted in John MacArthur, *The MacArthur New Testament Commentary: Ephesians* (Chicago: Moody Publishers, 1986), 53.

4. MacArthur, *New Testament Commentary: Ephesians*, 55.

5. *New Testament Greek Lexicon-NAS*, s.v. "kosmos," Bible Study Tools, accessed November 22, 2023, https://www.biblestudytools.com/lexicons/greek /nas/kosmos.html.

Chapter 5 Ego and Chasing Celebrity Status

1. *Cambridge Dictionary*, s.v. "ego," accessed November 22, 2023, https:// dictionary.cambridge.org/us/dictionary/english/ego.

2. Dictionary.com, s.v., "ego," accessed November 22, 2023, https://www .dictionary.com/browse/ego.

3. Chris Rojek, *Celebrity: Focus on Contemporary Issues* (London: Reaktion, 2001), loc. 48 of 3072, Kindle.

4. Ibid., 691 of 3072.

Chapter 6 The Demon of Distraction

1. *King James Bible Dictionary*, s.v. "distraction," accessed November 23, 2023, https://kingjamesbibledictionary.com/Dictionary/distraction.

2. Ibid.

3. Henry Morris, *The Genesis Record: A Scientific and Devotional Commentary on the Book of Beginnings* (Grand Rapids: Baker, 1976), 114.

4. Nick Cady, "Why Did Jesus Tell Some People to Keep Quiet about His Miracles and Identity?," Theology for the People, April 23, 2018, https://nick cady.org/2018/04/23/why-did-jesus-tell-some-people-to-keep-quiet-about-his -miracles-and-identity.

5. *Merriam-Webster Dictionary*, s.v. "sabotage," accessed November 23, 2023, https://www.merriam-webster.com/dictionary/sabotage.

6. *Benson Commentary*, "2 Samuel 12," Bible Hub, accessed November 23, 2023, https://biblehub.com/commentaries/benson/2_samuel/12.htm.

Chapter 7 Technology

1. Jason Thacker, *The Age of AI: Artificial Intelligence and the Future of Humanity* (Grand Rapids: Zondervan, 2020), 20.

2. Pamela Lassiter and Linda Fye, "Troposphere Definition, Characteristics & Temperature," Study.com, updated November 21, 2023, https://study.com /learn/lesson/troposphere-characteristics-temperature.html.

3. Sarah Clark and Dean Barjesteh, "The Information Superhighway: Data Transfer and Networking," University of Delaware (HTML conversion by George Watson), https://www.physics.udel.edu/~watson/scen103/projects/95f /voltage/project1-net.html.

4. Jeff Cranston, "Hedge of Protection," Jeff Cranston (blog), June 25, 2020, https://www.jeffcranston.com/blog/post/hedge-of-protection. (See also Bible Hub, s.v. "7753.suk," accessed November 23, 2023, https://biblehub.com/hebrew /7753.htm.)

5. Ibid.

6. Janis Heiser, "Hedge of Protection," *The Express*, July 27, 2019, https:// www.lockhaven.com/news/religion/2019/07/hedge-of-protection.

7. Cranston, "Hedge of Protection."

8. For more on the meaning of numbers in Scripture, see Jack Ashcraft, "What Is the Meaning of Numbers in the Bible and the Significance of Biblical Numerology?," Christianity.com, updated February 9, 2024, https://www.chris tianity.com/wiki/christian-terms/what-is-the-significance-of-biblical-numerol ogy.html.

9. Tony Reinke, *12 Ways Your Phone Is Changing You* (Carol Stream, Ill.: Crossway, 2017), 50.

10. "What Is Artificial Intelligence (AI)?," IBM, accessed November 23, 2023, https://www.ibm.com/topics/artificial-intelligence.

11. "Elon Musk Says Artificial Intelligence Is Like 'Summoning the Demon,'" CBS News, October 27, 2014, https://www.cbsnews.com/news/elon-musk-arti ficial-intelligence-is-like-summoning-the-demon.

12. Ibid.

13. "Protecting Americans from Foreign Adversary Controlled Applications Act," "H.R. 7521," 118th Cong., 2nd session, March 5, 2024, https://docs.house .gov/billsthisweek/20240311/HR%207521%20Updated.pdf.

14. "Facebook Quizzes Play on Your Emotions to Harvest Your Personal Data," Firebrand, accessed November 23, 2023, https://firebrand.net/facebook -quizzes-play-on-your-emotions-to-harvest-your-personal-data.

15. Rebecca Quinn, "What Was Apple's First Computer Price? (Explained)," The Cold Wire, May 7, 2022, https://www.thecoldwire.com/apple-first-computer -price.

16. Bobby Allyn, "How Microsoft's Experiment in Artificial Intelligence Tech Backfired," NPR, February 27, 2023, https://www.npr.org/2023/02/27 /1159630243/how-microsofts-experiment-in-artificial-intelligence-tech-back fired.

17. "An Unclean Spirit Used AI to Speak to My Son," YouTube video, 17:08, posted by Founded Earth Brothers, February 9, 2023, https://www.youtube.com /watch?v=15rwQ7ar3vE.

18. Ellen White, "Who Are the Nephilim?," Biblical Archaeology Society, January 30, 2024, https://www.biblicalarchaeology.org/daily/biblical-topics /hebrew-bible/who-are-the-nephilim.

19. Ron Cassie, "Not Dead Yet," *Baltimore* magazine, accessed November 23, 2023, https://www.baltimoremagazine.com/section/artsentertainment/the -dark-and-fascinating-history-of-the-ouija-board-baltimore-origins.

20. John Veal, "I'm in a Haunted House & See a Demon Doing This," You-Tube video, 24:19, posted by *Sid Roth's It's Supernatural!*, February 16, 2020, https://youtu.be/TGD1nr0XAlM.

21. Pat Brans, "What Is a daemon?" TechTarget, last updated August 2022, https://www.techtarget.com/whatis/definition/daemon#.

22. Dictionary.com, s.v. "The devil is in the details," accessed November 23, 2023, https://www.dictionary.com/browse/the-devil-is-in-the-details.

23. Poem Analysis, s.v. "The devil is in the details," accessed November 23, 2023, https://poemanalysis.com/proverb/the-devil-is-in-the-details.

Chapter 8 Destroying Demonic Tactics through Fasting and Prayer

1. Bible Study Tools, s.v. "Mattityahu 17:21," accessed November 24, 2023, https://www.biblestudytools.com/ojb/mattityahu/17-21.html.

2. "Tefillah," AlephBeta, accessed November 23, 2023, https://www.aleph beta.org/jewish-prayer/tefillah.

3. David Curwin, "Tzom and Ta'anit," *HaMizrachi* 3, no. 3 (July 2020): 31, https://mizrachi.org/wp-content/uploads/2020/07/HaMizrachi-Tisha-BAv-202 0_31.pdf.

4. This list of four kinds of biblical fasts is based on Melissa Tumino's list in her article "The 4 Types of Fasting in the Bible," Think about Such Things, accessed November 23, 2023, https://thinkaboutsuchthings.com/types-of-fasting -in-the-bible.

5. Ruth Brown, *Destroying the Works of Witchcraft through Fasting and Prayer* (Kirkwood, Mo.: Impact Christian Books, 1994), 34–36.

6. Rev. J. Patrick Street, "Pastor: Faith Moves God's Hand," *Marion Star*, March 30, 2019, https://www.marionstar.com/story/life/2019/03/30/pastor -faith-moves-gods-hand/3276440002.

7. *Merriam-Webster Dictionary*, s.v. "witch," accessed November 23, 2023, https://www.merriam-webster.com/dictionary/witch.

8. David F. Maas, "Fasting: Building Spiritual Muscle," Church of the Great God, August 2001, https://www.cgg.org/index.cfm/library/article/id/5/fasting -building-spiritual-muscle.htm.

9. New American Standard New Testament Greek Lexicon, s.v. "dunamis" (Strong's 1411), accessed November 23, 2023, https://www.biblestudytools.com /lexicons/greek/nas/dunamis.html.

10. New American Standard New Testament Greek Lexicon, s.v. "exousia" (Strong's 1849), accessed November 23, 2023, https://www.biblestudytools.com /lexicons/greek/nas/exousia.html.

11. KJV Dictionary, s.v. "fortress," AV1611, accessed November 23, 2023, https://av1611.com/kjbp/kjv-dictionary/fortress.html.

Chapter 9 Avoiding Hazardous Environments

1. *The Pursuit of Happyness*, YouTube video, 1:57:12, posted by Kunal Newatia, November 12, 2012, https://www.youtube.com/watch?v=8fnVG-EKFmE.

2. Cynde Layne Wilkerson, "Disturbers of Our Harmony," *Morning Love* (blog), March 2011, http://cyndesmorninglove.blogspot.com/2011/03/disturbers -of-our-harmony.html.

3. A. W. Tozer, *The Alliance Weekly/Witness* (1960), quoted in *The Quotable Tozer: A Topical Compilation of the Wisdom and Insight of A. W. Tozer* (Minneapolis: Bethany House, 2018), 105.

4. Word by Word Bible Study, "Satan in the Bible: 14 Sobering Facts about the Devil," Logos, August 17, 2021, https://www.logos.com/grow/Satan-in-the -bible.

5. Doug Batchelor and Jëan Ross, "The Cuckoo Bird Deception," *Bible Answers Live*, 59:53, January 23, 2011, https://www.amazingfacts.org/media -library/media/e/2373/f/6/t/the-cuckoo-bird-deception.

6. New American Standard New Testament Greek Lexicon, s.v. "tachus," Bible Study Tools, accessed November 24, 2023, https://www.biblestudytools .com/lexicons/greek/nas/tachus.html.

7. Dictionary.com, s.v. "third eye," accessed November 24, 2023, https://www.dictionary.com/browse/third-eye.

8. Ibid.

9. *Merriam-Webster Dictionary*, s.v. "twerking," accessed November 24, 2023, https://www.merriam-webster.com/dictionary/twerking.

Chapter 10 You Will Prevail!

1. "Jacob," Behind the Name, accessed November 24, 2023, https://www.behindthename.com/name/jacob.

2. Daniel E. Anderson, "Origin of the Word *Yosemite*," Yosemite Online, last updated July 2011, https://www.yosemite.ca.us/library/origin_of_word_yosemite.html.

3. Bruce Goettsche, as quoted in the blog "Wrestling with God," *Veritas Ministeria*, July 3, 2012, https://thetruth-blog.blogspot.com/2012/07/wrestling-with-god.html.

4. Bruce Goettsche, "Jacob Takes Up Wrestling—Genesis 32," Sermons by Logos, August 11, 2019, https://sermons.logos.com/sermons/601174-jacob-takes-up-wrestling-genesis-32.

5. Ibid.

6. *Merriam-Webster Dictionary*, s.v. "Sanhedrin," accessed November 24, 2023, https://www.merriam-webster.com/dictionary/Sanhedrin.

JOHN VEAL is the senior pastor/prophet of Enduring Faith Christian Center and the CEO of John Veal Ministries, Inc. He is a regular contributor to *Charisma* magazine, The Elijah List, Spirit Fuel, and more. He has also been featured in *iMAG, Rejoice Essential, Reformation Today,* and other magazines.

John has been featured on various media outlets, including *Sid Roth's It's Supernatural!,* ISN's *Something More, ElijahStreams, Glory Road TV,* God TV, and *The Shaun Tabatt Show.* Due to his uncanny prophetic accuracy, humor, candor, and unconventional preaching style, he is also a highly sought-after conference speaker. He has traveled the nations, passionate about pursuing God's mandate to preach, teach, impart, and activate people within the prophetic and train them in deliverance.

John is a certified teacher with the Chicago Board of Education, and is also a licensed real estate managing broker. He holds a master's degree in special education from Dominican University, and a master's degree in educational leadership from American College of Education. Dr. Veal also received an honorary doctorate in theology and ministry from Healing Waters Biblical

Institute & Seminary. He currently resides in Chicago, Illinois, with his wife, Elisa, and their three daughters. To find out more about John and his ministry, or to sign up for his online course "Hearing Navigation":

www.JohnVeal.org

www.JohnVealSchool.org/courses/hearingnavigation

www.Faith2Endure.com
(Enduring Faith Christian Center's website)

John also hosts two podcasts you can listen to:

The Prophetic Pour with John Veal
(Charisma Podcast Network)

Supernaturally Prophetic with John Veal
(Destiny Image)

Find John on social media:

@ProphetVeal (personal page)

@ProphetJV (public page)

@groups/SupernaturallyProphetic

@ProphetJohnVeal

@JohnVeal9114